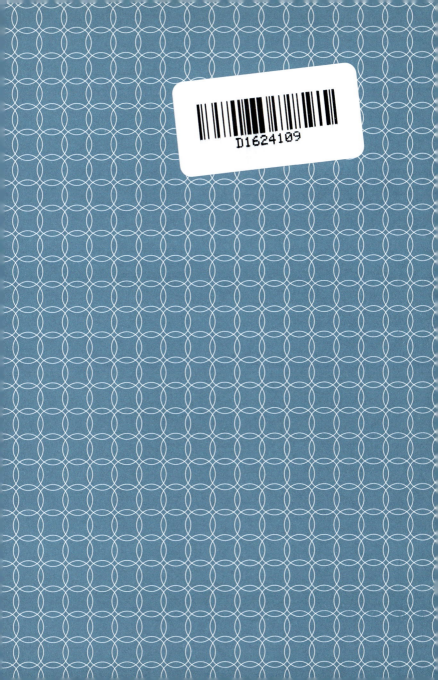

CONSCIOUSNESS

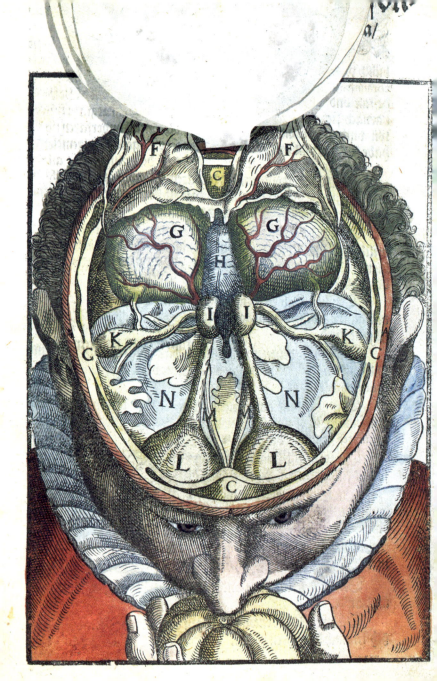

CONSCIOUSNESS

Susan Blackmore

A BRIEF INSIGHT

STERLING

New York / London
www.sterlingpublishing.com

STERLING and the distinctive Sterling logo are registered trademarks of
Sterling Publishing Co., Inc.

Library of Congress Cataloging-in-Publication Data Available

10 9 8 7 6 5 4 3 2 1

Published by Sterling Publishing Co., Inc.
387 Park Avenue South, New York, NY 10016

Published by arrangement with Oxford University Press, Inc.

Distributed in Canada by Sterling Publishing
c/o Canadian Manda Group, 165 Dufferin Street
Toronto, Ontario, Canada M6K 3H6

Book design: The DesignWorks Group

Please see picture credits on page 184 for image copyright information.

Printed in China

Sterling ISBN 978-1-4027-7528-4

For information about custom editions, special sales, premium and corporate purchases, please contact
Sterling Special Sales Department at 800-805-5489 or specialsales@sterlingpublishing.com.

Frontispiece: This woodblock print of the brain appeared in German physician Georg Bartisch's
Ophthalmodouleia das ist Augendienst, published in Dresden in 1583.

CONTENTS

•

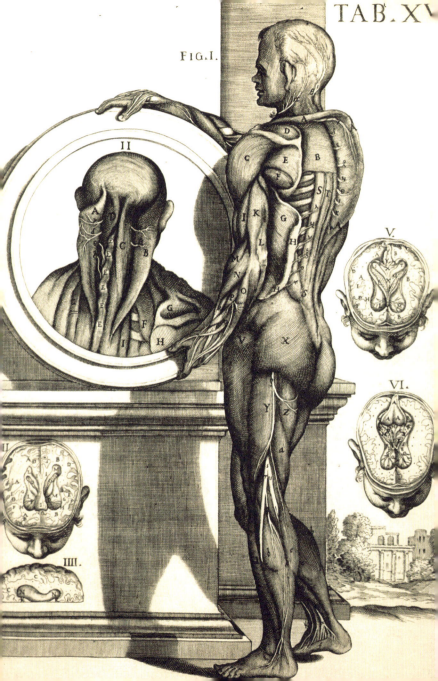

TAB. XV

FIG. I.

ONE

Why the Mystery?

•

The Hard Problem

What is consciousness? This may sound like a simple question but it is not. Consciousness is at once the most obvious and the most difficult thing we can investigate. We seem either to have to use consciousness to investigate itself, which is a slightly weird idea, or to have to extricate ourselves from the very thing we want to study. No wonder that philosophers and scientists have struggled for millennia with the concept, and that scientists rejected the whole idea for long periods and refused even to study it. The good news is that, at the start of the twenty-first century,

Philosophers and scientists have struggled with the concept of consciousness for millennia, but only now do we know enough about the brain to confront the question head-on. This engraving of the anatomy of the human male including several cutaway drawings of the brain is from *Tabulae anatomicae* (published posthumously in 1741) by Italian artist and architect Pietro da Cortona (1596–1669).

"consciousness studies" is thriving. Psychology, biology, and neuroscience have reached the point when they are ready to confront some tricky questions: What does consciousness do? Could we have evolved without it? Could consciousness be an illusion? What is consciousness, anyway?

This does not mean that the mystery has gone away. Indeed, it is as deep as ever. The difference now is that we know enough about the brain to be ready to confront the problem head-on. How on earth can the electrical firing of millions of tiny brain cells produce this—my private, subjective, conscious experience?

If we are going to get anywhere with understanding consciousness, we have to take this problem seriously. There are many people who claim to have solved the mystery of consciousness: they propose grand unifying theories, quantum mechanical theories, spiritual theories of the "power of consciousness," and many more, but most of them simply ignore the yawning chasm, or "fathomless abyss," between the physical and mental worlds. As long as they ignore this problem they are not really dealing with consciousness at all.

This problem is a modern incarnation of the famous mind–body problem with which philosophers have struggled for more than two thousand years. The trouble is that in ordinary human experience there seem to be two entirely different kinds of thing, with no obvious way to bring the two together.

On the one hand, there are our own experiences. Right now I can see the houses and trees on a distant hill, hear the cars down on the main road, enjoy the warmth and familiarity of my own room, and wonder whether that scratching noise is the cat wanting to be let in. All of these are my own private experiences and they have a quality that I cannot convey to anyone else. I may wonder whether your experience of green is the same as mine or whether coffee has exactly the same smell for you as it does for me, but I can never find out. These ineffable (or indescribable) qualities are what philosophers call "qualia" (although there is much dispute about whether qualia exist). The redness of that shiny red mug is a quale; the soft feel of my cat's fur is a quale; and so is that smell of coffee. These experiences seem to be real, vivid, and undeniable. They make up the world I live in. Indeed, they are all I have.

On the other hand, I really do believe that there exists a physical world out there that gives rise to these experiences. I may have doubts about what it is made of, or about its deeper nature, but I do not doubt that it exists. If I denied its existence I would not be able to explain why, if I go to the door, I shall probably see the cat rushing in—and if you came by you would agree that there was now a cat trailing muddy footprints across my desk.

The trouble is that these two kinds of thing seem to be utterly different. There are real physical things with size, shape, weight, and other attributes that everyone can measure and agree upon, and then there are private experiences—the feeling of pain, the color of that apple as I see it now.

Throughout history most people have adopted some kind of dualism: that is, the belief that there are indeed two different realms or worlds. This is true of most non-Western cultures today, and surveys suggest that it is true of most educated Westerners as well. The major religions are almost all dualist: Christians and Muslims believe in an eternal, nonphysical soul, and Hindus believe in the atman or divine self within. Among religions, Buddhism alone rejects the idea of a persisting inner self or soul. Even among nonreligious people, dualism is prevalent in Western cultures. Popular New Age theories invoke the powers of mind,

Most people from most cultures are dualist, as are the major religions. That is, they believe that mind and brain occupy two different realms. "Dr. Alford's Biblical Chart of Man," a late-nineteenth-century lithograph by the Rev. L. A. Alford, an Indianan Baptist clergyman, purports to show the relation of the soul to the body, the senses to the attributes, and mortality to immortality.

consciousness, or spirit, as though they were an independent force; and alternative therapists champion the effect of mind on body, as though these were two separate things. Such dualism is so deeply embedded in our language that we may happily refer to "my brain" or "my body," as though "I" am something separate from "them."

In the seventeenth century the French philosopher René Descartes (1596–1650) formally proposed the best-known dualist theory. Known as Cartesian dualism, this is the idea that the mind and the brain consist of different substances. According to Descartes, the mind is nonphysical and nonextended (i.e., it takes up no space or has no position), while the body and the rest of the physical world are made of physical, or extended, substance. The trouble with this is obvious. How do the two interact? Descartes proposed that they meet in the tiny pineal gland in the center of the brain, but this only staves off the problem a little. The pineal gland is a physical structure, and Cartesian dualism provides no explanation of why it, alone, can communicate with the mental realm.

Seventeenth-century French philosopher René Descartes is the author of the best-known dualist theory, that the mind and the brain consist of different substances, with the pineal gland their point of interaction.

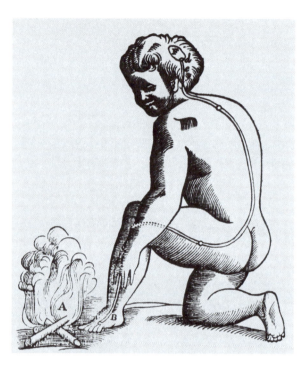

Descartes explained reflex responses to pain in terms of mechanical responses and the flow of "animal spirits" in tiny tubes. But when it came to conscious experiences he proposed that they were part of a quite different mental world, connected to the physical body through the pineal gland in the center of the brain.

This problem of interaction bedevils any attempt to build a dualist theory, which is probably why most philosophers and scientists completely reject all forms of dualism in favor of some kind of monism; but the options are few and also problematic. Idealists make mind fundamental but must then explain why and how there appears to be a consistent physical world. Neutral monists reject dualism but disagree about the fundamental nature of the world and how to unify it. A third option is materialism, and this is by far the most popular among scientists today. Materialists take matter as fundamental, but they must then face the problem that this book is all about. How do you account for consciousness? How can a physical brain, made purely of material substances and nothing else, give rise to conscious experiences or ineffable qualia?

This problem is called the "hard problem" of consciousness, a phrase coined in 1994 by the Australian philosopher David Chalmers. He wanted to distinguish this serious and overwhelming difficulty from what he called the "easy problems." The easy problems, according to Chalmers, are those that in principle we know how to solve, even if we have not yet done so. They include such problems as perception, learning, attention, or memory; how we discriminate objects or react to stimuli; how sleep differs from being awake. All these are easy, he says, compared with the really hard problem of experience itself.

Not everyone agrees with Chalmers. Some claim that the hard problem does not exist; that it depends on a false conception of consciousness, or on drastically underestimating the "easy" problems. The American philosopher Patricia Churchland calls it a "hornswoggle problem," arguing that we cannot, in advance, decide which problems will turn out to be the really hard ones. It arises, she claims, from the false intuition that if we explained perception, memory, attention, and all the other details, there would still be something left out—"consciousness itself."

These are important objections. So before we go any further we must be clearer about what, if anything, "consciousness itself" might mean.

Defining Consciousness

What is it like to be a bat? This curious question looms large in the history of consciousness studies. First asked in the 1950s, it was made famous by

American philosopher Thomas Nagel posed the question, "What is it like to be a bat?" to explore what is meant by consciousness. He chose bats because their experience of the world, "seen" by echolocation, must be so different from ours. This photograph of a bat in flight appeared in F. Chanut's article on echolocation, "The Sound of Dinner," *PLoS Biology* 4, no. 4 (March 7, 2006).

the American philosopher Thomas Nagel in 1974. He used the question to challenge materialism, to explore what we mean by consciousness, and to see why it makes the mind–body problem so intractable. What we mean, he said, is *subjectivity*. If there is something it is like to be the bat—something *for the bat itself*, then the bat is conscious. If there is nothing it is like to be the bat, then it is not.

· · · · ·

DEFINING CONSCIOUSNESS

There is no generally agreed definition of consciousness, but the following gives some idea of what is meant by the word.

"What it's like to be . . .": If there is something it is like to be an animal (or computer, or baby) then that thing is conscious. Otherwise it is not.

Subjectivity or phenomenality: Consciousness means subjective experience or phenomenal experience. This is the way things seem to me, as opposed to how they are objectively.

Qualia: The ineffable subjective qualities of experience, such as the redness of red or the indescribable smell of turpentine. Some philosophers claim they do not exist.

The hard problem: How do subjective experiences arise from objective brains?

· · · · ·

So think, for example, of the mug, or pot, or plastic ornament on your table. Now ask—what is it like to be the mug? You will probably answer that it is like nothing at all; that mugs cannot feel, that china is inert, and so on. You will probably have no trouble in opining that pots and mugs are not conscious. But move on to worms, flies, bacteria, or bats and you may have more trouble. You do not know—indeed, you cannot know—what it is like to be an earthworm. Even so, as Nagel points out, if you think that there is something it is like to be the worm then you believe that the worm is conscious.

Nagel chose the bat as his example because bats are so very different from us. They fly, live mostly in the dark, hang upside-down from trees or in damp caves, and use sonar, not vision, to see the world. That is, they emit rapid bursts of high-pitched squeaks while they fly, and then, by analyzing the echoes that come back to their sensitive ears, learn about the world around them.

What is it like to experience the world this way? It is no good imagining that you are a bat because an educated, speaking bat would not be a normal bat at all; conversely, if *you* became a normal bat and could not think or speak then you would not be able to answer your own question.

Nagel argued that we can never know and from this concluded that the problem is insoluble. For this reason he is dubbed a mysterian. Another mysterian is the American philosopher Colin McGinn, who argues that we humans are "cognitively closed" with respect to understanding consciousness. That is, we have no hope of understanding consciousness, just as a dog has no hope of being able to read the newspaper he so happily carries back from the shops. Psychologist Stephen Pinker agrees: we may be able to understand most of the detail of how the mind works, yet consciousness itself may remain forever beyond our reach.

Not many people share Nagel's pessimism, but his question has proved helpful in reminding us what is at stake when we talk about consciousness. It is no good talking about perception, memory, intelligence, or problem solving as purely physical processes and then claiming to have explained consciousness. If you are really talking about consciousness, then you must deal in some way or another with subjectivity. Either you must actually solve the hard problem and explain how subjectivity arises from the material world, or alternatively, if you claim that consciousness is identical to those physical processes, or is an illusion or even that it does not exist at all, you must explain why it *appears* so strongly to exist. Either way, you can only claim to be dealing with consciousness if you are talking about "What it is like to be . . ."

This essential meaning of the term *consciousness* is also called *phenomenality*, or *phenomenal consciousness*, terms coined by American philosopher Ned Block. Block compares *phenomenal consciousness*, which is what it is like to be in a certain state, with *access consciousness*, which refers to availability for use in thinking, or guiding action and speech. Phenomenal consciousness (or phenomenality, or subjectivity) is what Nagel was talking about and is the core of the problem of consciousness.

With these ideas in mind, we are ready for one of the central disputes in consciousness studies. This concerns the following question: Is consciousness an extra ingredient that we humans have in addition to our abilities of perceiving, thinking, and feeling, or is it an intrinsic and inseparable part of being a creature that can perceive and think and feel? This really is the key question on which the rest depends, and you might like to decide now what you think about it, for the implications either way are quite striking.

On the one hand, if consciousness is an extra added ingredient, then we naturally want to ask why we have it. We want to ask what consciousness is for, what it does, and how we got it. In this view, it is easy to imagine that we might have evolved without it, and so we want to know why consciousness evolved, what advantages it gave us, and whether it evolved in other creatures too. In this view, the hard problem is indeed hard; and the task ahead is to answer these difficult questions.

On the other hand, if consciousness is intrinsic to complex brain processes and inseparable from them, then it is nonsensical to ask most of these questions. In this view (which in some versions is called functionalism), there is no use in asking why consciousness evolved, because any creature that evolved to have intelligence, perception, memory, and emotions would necessarily be conscious as well. Also there would be no sense in talking about "consciousness itself" or about "ineffable qualia," for there is nothing extra that exists apart from the processes and abilities.

In this view, there really is no deep mystery, and no hard problem. So the task is quite different; it is to explain why there seems to be such a problem and why we *seem* to be having ineffable, nonphysical, conscious experiences. It is here that the idea of consciousness as an illusion comes in, for neither consciousness nor the hard problem is what it seems, and so we must explain how the illusion comes about.

If the implications of this dichotomy seem hard to grasp, a thought experiment might help.

Zombie

Imagine someone who looks exactly like you, acts like you, thinks like you, and speaks like you, but who is not conscious at all. This other you has no private, conscious experiences; all its actions are carried out without the light of awareness. This unconscious creature—not some half-dead Haitian corpse—is what philosophers mean by a zombie.

Zombies are certainly easy to imagine, but could they really exist? This apparently simple question leads to a whole world of philosophical difficulties.

When philosophers talk about zombies, they mean someone who looks just like a person but has no private, conscious experience—not a half-dead Haitian corpse.

On the "yes" side are those who believe that it really is possible to have two functionally equivalent systems, one of which is conscious while the other is unconscious. Chalmers is on the "yes" side. He claims that zombies are not only imaginable but possible— in some other world if not in this one. He imagines his zombie twin who behaves exactly like the real Chalmers but has no conscious experiences, no inner world, and no qualia. All is dark inside the mind of zombie-Dave. Other philosophers have dreamed up thought experiments involving a zombie earth populated by zombie people, or speculated that some real-live philosophers might actually be zombies pretending to be conscious.

On the "no" side are those who believe the whole idea of zombies is absurd, including both Churchland and American philosopher Daniel Dennett. The idea is ridiculous, they claim, because any system that could walk, talk, think, play games, choose what to wear, enjoy a good dinner, and do all the other things that we do would necessarily have to be conscious. The trouble is, they complain, that when people imagine a zombie they cheat: they do not take the definition seriously enough. So if you don't want to cheat, remember that the zombie has to be completely indistinguishable from a normal person on the outside. That is, it is no good asking the zombie questions about its experiences or testing its philosophy, for *by definition* it must behave just as a conscious person would. If you really follow the rules, the critics say, the idea disappears into nonsense.

It should now be easy to see that the zombie is really just a vivid way to think about the key question: Is consciousness a special added extra that we conscious humans are lucky to have, or is it something that necessarily comes along with all those evolved skills of perceiving, thinking, and feeling? If you believe that it's an added extra, then you can believe that we might all have evolved as zombies instead of as conscious people—and even that your neighbor might be a zombie. But if you believe that it's intrinsic and inseparable from the skills we humans have, then zombies simply could not exist and the whole idea is daft.

I think the whole idea is daft. Nevertheless, it remains extremely alluring, largely because it is so easy to imagine a zombie. Yet how easy something is to imagine is not a good guide to its truth. So let's consider a rather different aspect of the same problem—the question of whether consciousness does anything.

The phrase *the power of consciousness* is common in popular discourse. The idea is that consciousness is some sort of force that can directly influence the world—either by acting on our own bodies, as when "I" consciously decide to move my arm and it moves—or, more controversially, in things like psychic healing, telepathy, or "mind over matter." Like the zombie, this "power" is easy to imagine. We can visualize our conscious mind somehow reaching out and influencing things. But does this idea make any sense? As soon as you remember that consciousness means subjectivity or phenomenality, then the idea begins to seem less plausible. How could "what it's like to be" something be a force or power? How could my experience of the green of that tree cause something to happen?

One way to explore whether consciousness could be a power or force is to ask what would happen if you took it away. Obviously, if consciousness has any power at all, what would be left could not be a zombie because the zombie must, by definition, be indistinguishable from a conscious person. So you would be left with someone who was different from a conscious person because they could not . . . what?

Perhaps you think consciousness is needed for making decisions, but we know a lot about how the brain makes decisions, and it does not seem to need an extra added force to do so. Also, we can make computers that make decisions without a special consciousness module. The same goes for seeing, hearing, controlling movements, and many other human abilities. Perhaps you think it is needed for aesthetic appreciation, creativity, or falling in love, but, if so, you would have to show that these things are done by consciousness itself rather than by the workings of a clever brain.

All this leads to the awkward notion that perhaps consciousness does nothing, and other oddities point the same way. For example, think about people catching cricket balls, playing table tennis, or interrupting fast-flowing conversations. These quick actions all seem to be done consciously, but is it the consciousness itself that makes them happen? In fact, as we shall see, such actions happen too fast, and they are coordinated by parts of the brain that appear not to be involved in conscious experience.

Consciousness is not necessary for making decisions. We know a lot about how the brain makes decisions, and we can make computers that make decisions, and neither needs a special consciousness module. A popular early example of a decision-making computer is IBM's Deep Blue, which lost a chess match to chess champion Garry Kasparov in 1996 but won the rematch, shown in this photograph taken on May 5, 1997.

Could consciousness, then, be completely powerless? One version of this idea is epiphenomenalism—the idea that consciousness is a useless by-product or epiphenomenon. This is a very curious notion because it entails consciousness actually existing but having no effects on anything else. And if it has no effects at all it is hard to see how we could end up worrying about it—or even talking about it.

But epiphenomenalism is not the only way of understanding consciousness as powerless. An alternative is to say that all creatures like us that can see, feel, think, fall in love, and appreciate a fine wine will inevitably end up believing they are conscious, imagining zombies are possible, and thinking that consciousness does things. The bottom line for this kind of theory is that we are deluded; we feel as though consciousness is a power or added ability, but we are wrong. If this theory needs a name, we might call it "delusionism."

I think this is the right way to think about consciousness, but it implies that our ordinary assumptions about consciousness are deeply misguided. Could we really be so wrong? And why should we be? Perhaps we should take a closer look at some of those assumptions and ask how reliable they are.

The Theater of the Mind

The most natural way to think about consciousness is probably something like this. The mind feels like a private theater. Here I am, inside the theater, located roughly somewhere inside my head and looking out through my eyes. But this is a multisensational theater. So I experience touches, smells, sounds, and emotions as well. And I can use my imagination too—conjuring up sights and sounds to be seen as though on a mental screen by my inner eye or heard by my inner ear. All these are the "contents of my consciousness" and "I" am the audience of one who experiences them.

This theater imagery fits happily with another common image of consciousness—that it flows like a river or stream. In the nineteenth century, the "father of modern psychology," William James (1842–1910), coined the phrase *the stream of consciousness*, and it seems apt enough. Our conscious life really does feel like a continuously flowing stream of sights, sounds, smells, touches, thoughts, emotions, worries, and joys—all of which happen, one after another, to me.

This way of conceiving of our own minds is so easy, and so natural, that it hardly seems worth questioning. Yet when we get into an

American philosopher William James, whose term *stream of consciousness* first appeared in his *Principles of Psychology*, appears here in a photograph taken in September 1909 at a celebration of the Psychological Department at Clark University in Worcester, Massachusetts. James is in the first row, third from left, holding his hat and coat.

intellectual muddle, as we seem to have done with the problem of consciousness, it is sometimes worth challenging our most basic assumptions—in this case, these apparently innocent analogies.

The strongest challenge comes from philosopher Daniel Dennett. He argues that while most people are happy to reject the idea of Cartesian dualism, they still retain strong vestiges of dualist thinking in the form of what he calls the Cartesian theater. This is not just the analogy of the mind with a theater, but the notion that somewhere in the mind or brain there must be a place and time at which everything comes together and "consciousness happens," that there is some kind of finishing line in the brain's activities, after which things mysteriously become conscious or "enter consciousness."

This has to be false, claims Dennett. To begin with, there is no center in the brain which could correspond to this notion, for the brain is a radically parallel processing system with no central headquarters. Information comes in to the senses and is distributed all over the place for different purposes. In all of this activity there is no central place in which "I" sit and watch the show as things pass through my consciousness. There is no place in which the arrival of thoughts or perceptions marks the moment at which they become conscious. There is no single location from where my decisions are sent out. Instead, the many different parts

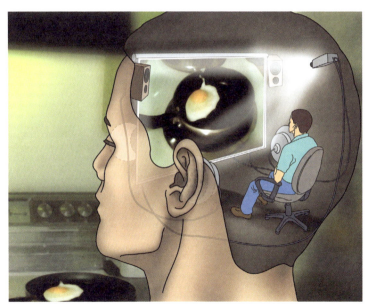

I feel as though I am somewhere inside my head looking out—that I experience the outside world through my eyes and ears, imagine things in my mind's eye, and direct my arms and legs to walk me into the kitchen to make my breakfast. But the brain cannot work this way. This is Dennett's mythical Cartesian theater.

American philosopher Daniel Dennett, shown here in his office at Tufts University in November 2005, rejects the ideas of both the Cartesian theater and Cartesian materialism, claiming that there is no central place in the brain where information comes together and becomes conscious.

of the brain just get on with their own jobs, communicating with one another whenever necessary, and with no central control. What, then, could correspond to the theater of consciousness?

It is no good, adds Dennett, to shift from thinking of the theater as an actual place, to thinking of it as some kind of distributed process, or widespread neural network. The principle remains the same and is still wrong. There simply is no place or process or anything else that corresponds to the conscious bit of the brain's activities, leaving all the rest unconscious. There is no sense in which the input is brought together to be displayed "in consciousness" for someone to see or hear, and no little person inside who acts on what they see. The brain is not organized that way, and it wouldn't work if it were. Somehow we have to understand how this feeling of being a conscious self having a stream of experiences comes about in a brain that really has no inner theater, no show, and no audience.

Dennett coined the term *Cartesian materialist* to describe those scientists who claim to reject dualism but still believe in the Cartesian theater. Note that both these terms, *Cartesian theater* and *Cartesian materialism*, are Dennett's and not Descartes's. Few, if any, scientists admit to being Cartesian materialists. Yet, as we shall see, the vast majority assume something like a stream of consciousness, or treat the mind as an inner theater. They may, of course, be right, and if they are, then the task of a science of consciousness is to explain what that metaphorical theater corresponds to in the brain and how it works. But I rather doubt that they are. Exploring a little more about how the brain works may help us to see why.

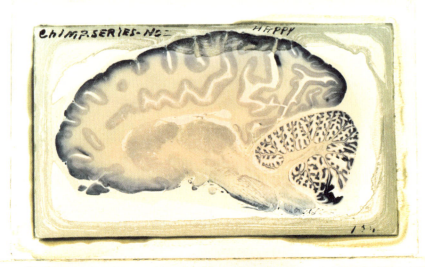

CHIMP. SERIES. No.   HAPPY

130.

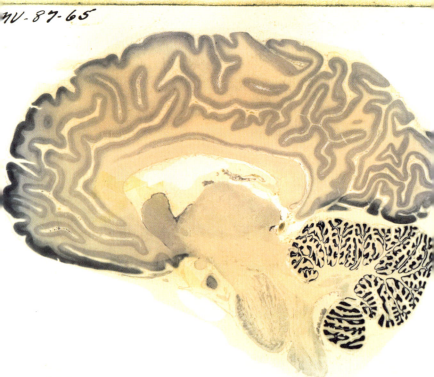

TWO

The Human Brain

•

The Unity of Consciousness

The human brain is said to be the most complex object in the known universe. Relative to body weight, human brains are larger than those of any other species, and by a long way. They are about three times larger than you would expect by comparing them with those of our closest relatives, the other great apes. A human brain weighs nearly three pounds (one and a half kilograms) and consists of more than a billion neurons (nerve cells), with many billions of interconnections. Out of all these connections come our extraordinary abilities: perception, learning, memory, reasoning, language, and—somehow or another—consciousness.

Relative to body weight, the human brain is about three times larger than you would expect it to be, if you compared it to the brains of the other great apes. This image shows a comparison of human and chimpanzee brains at the National Museum of Health and Medicine in Washington, D.C.

We know that the brain is intimately involved in consciousness because changes in the brain cause changes in consciousness. For example, drugs that affect brain function also affect subjective experiences; stimulation of small areas of the brain can induce specific experiences such as hallucinations, physical sensations, or emotional reactions; and damage to the brain can drastically affect a person's state of consciousness. This much we know for sure, but what remains a mystery is why we should be conscious at all.

In some ways the brain does not seem to be designed the right way to produce the kind of consciousness we have. Most characteristically the brain is massively parallel and distributed in its design. Information comes in through the senses and is used to control speech, actions, and

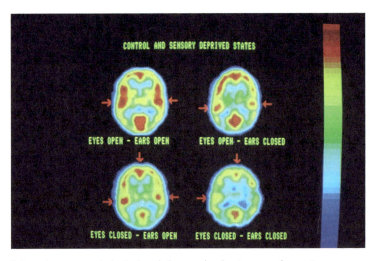

Information comes to the brain through the senses, but there is no central processing system. This color-coded result of a brain-stimulation test, made with a PET scanner, shows the different parts of the brain that become active (in red) under various conditions.

other outputs, but there is no central organization, no inner sanctum where the really important bits happen. A brain is more like a vast network—or a vast collection of interpenetrating networks—than like a personal computer with a central processor. Nothing is centralized in the human brain. Different areas deal with vision, hearing, speech, body image, motor control, forward planning, and countless other tasks. They are all linked up to one another, but this is not done by sending everything into one central processor, but by having millions of crisscrossing connections running all over the place.

By contrast, human consciousness seems to be unified. This "unity of consciousness" is often described in three distinct ways—and the natural way of thinking about consciousness, in terms of a theater or a stream of experiences, implies all three.

First, it implies that at any particular time, there is a unity to those things I am experiencing now; that is, some things are in my consciousness while many others are not. Those inside are called the "contents of consciousness" and form the current experiences in the stream or the show on the stage of the theater. Second, consciousness seems unified over time in that there seems to be a continuity from one moment to the next, or even across a whole lifetime of conscious experiences. Third, these conscious contents are experienced by the same "me." In other words, there is a single experiencer as well as the stream of experiences.

A successful science of consciousness must therefore explain the contents of consciousness, the continuity of consciousness, and the self who is conscious, and it must do so starting with a multiply parallel and noncentralized brain. We shall return to the question of self, but for now let's begin with the apparently innocent idea that there are contents of consciousness.

The important point here is that most of what goes on in the human brain seems to be outside of consciousness and even inaccessible to consciousness. We see the trees blowing in the wind, but we are not conscious of all the rapid electrical activity in the visual cortex that leads up to that perception. We sit at our computer consciously replying to an e-mail, but are unconscious of how our hands type the words or where the words are coming from. We consciously struggle to win that game of table tennis, oblivious to the fast visuo-motor control that makes our winning shots possible.

In all these cases every one of our brain's cells, with their billions of connections, are active—some firing faster and some slower, depending on what we are doing. Yet most of this activity never makes it into the stream of consciousness or the theater of my mind. So we call it unconscious or subconscious, or we relegate it to the fringe of consciousness.

But what does this really mean? The problem is that this distinction implies a magic difference between the conscious bits and the unconscious bits. Is the conscious brain activity controlled by a supernatural soul or nonphysical self, as a dualist might believe? Is there a special place in the brain where consciousness happens? Are there special types of "consciousness neuron" that produce conscious experiences while all the rest do not? Are there certain ways of connecting up neurons that produce consciousness? Or what? As we shall see, there are theories of consciousness corresponding to all these possibilities, but all of them face severe difficulties.

In the end, the question seems to be this—do we struggle on with the familiar view of consciousness as a theater or stream of experiences and try to make it work, or do we throw out all our familiar ways of thinking and begin again? It is worth bearing this question in mind as we consider some of the fascinating research that links consciousness to brain function.

· · · · ·

SYNESTHESIA

Some people hear shapes, see noises, or feel sounds, and this odd form of unified consciousness is surprisingly common. Many young children have synesthesia but the effects usually disappear with age, leaving something like one in two hundred adults as synesthetes. Synesthesia runs in families, is more common in women and left-handers, and is associated with good memory but poorer math and spatial ability. It is especially prevalent among poets, writers, and artists.

In the most common form of synesthesia, numbers or letters are always seen as colored. These experiences cannot be consciously suppressed, and when tested after many years most synesthetes report that exactly the same shapes or forms or colors are induced by the same stimuli. Many synesthetes hide their abilities, and for a long time psychologists doubted they were real, but recent research has confirmed the prevalence and stability of the effects.

Synesthetes may have more connections between the different sensory areas of the brain, and Ramachandran argues that since numbers and color are processed in adjacent areas this might explain the most common form of synesthesia.

· · · · ·

The Neural Correlates of Consciousness (NCCs)

Everyone has experienced pain. Pain is horrid. It hurts and we don't like it. But what is it? Pain is a perfect example for considering the neural correlates of consciousness; that is, the brain events that are correlated, or associated, with subjective experiences.

On the subjective side, pain is quintessentially a private experience. We cannot describe our pain to anyone else. We cannot know how bad someone else's pain is, except by watching the person's behavior, and even then we might think that he or she is bluffing, although we can never be sure. We cannot even remember how pain feels once it is gone. Indeed, it is often said that no woman would ever have a second baby if she could remember the pain of the first. In the end, the only way we can really know what pain is like is when we are suffering it now.

On the objective side, pain happens when, for example, the body is injured. Various chemical changes take place at the site of the injury, and then signals pass along specialized neurons called C-fibers to the spinal cord, and from there to the brain stem, thalamus, somatosensory cortex (which includes a map of all the areas of the body), and cingulate cortex of the brain. Brain scans show that there is a strong correlation between the amount of pain experienced and the amount of activity in these areas. In other words, we understand some of the neural correlates of pain.

Now, it is important to remember that "correlation does not imply a cause." It is notoriously easy to slip from correlations to false conclusions about causes, as in this simple example. Suppose that Freddie has a habit of going into the living room and turning on the television. Almost every time he does so, his action is soon followed by *The Simpsons* coming on. When other people go into the living room and press the button, completely different things come on. If correlation implied cause, then we would have to conclude that Freddie's action caused *The Simpsons* to appear. In this case, of course, we are not fooled. But in many other cases we might be.

The rule of thumb to remember is this: Whenever there is a reliable correlation between A and B, there are three possible causal explanations: A caused B, B caused A, or A and B were both caused by something else. In addition, it could be that A and B are actually the same thing even though they do not appear to be (like water and H_2O, or the morning star and the evening star).

Which is the case with pain? Maybe the physical changes *cause* the pain, in which case we have to solve the hard problem. Maybe the pain causes the physical changes, in which case we need a supernatural theory. Maybe something else causes both, in which case we have no idea what. Or maybe they are really the same thing. Many materialists have argued for this last explanation, but if it is true we have absolutely no idea how it could be true. How could this awful, toe-curling, horrible, unwanted feeling in the side of my head actually be the firing of a few of my C-fibers?

This question illustrates the depth of our present ignorance about consciousness, but we should not despair. Science has a habit of solving what seem to be impossible problems and may do so again. So let's look at an example of some very clever experiments designed to delve into the neural correlates of consciousness—in this case, visual consciousness.

Look at the Necker cube on page 30. As you keep looking, the cube will flip between two different possible interpretations; you may even be able to make this happen deliberately. It feels as though first one view comes into consciousness and then the other, as though the two views are competing for consciousness.

Ambiguous figures like this provide an ideal opportunity to study the neural correlates of particular experiences. For example, we might be able to find which parts of the brain change when the experience flips, and that might mean that we had found the place where the perceptions enter consciousness—or identified the special consciousness neurons—or located the center of visual awareness.

In the 1980s, the Greek biologist Nikos Logothetis devised experiments with monkeys to test just this. He used a different kind of ambiguity called binocular rivalry in which different pictures are shown to the two eyes. In this situation, the two pictures compete for consciousness, as with the Necker cube. Monkeys apparently respond the same way as we do, for they are able to press a lever to say which picture they are currently seeing. So Logothetis inserted electrodes in different parts of their brains, including the early part of the visual cortex (V1), later visual areas (V4), and parts of the temporal cortex where some visual information goes after the initial

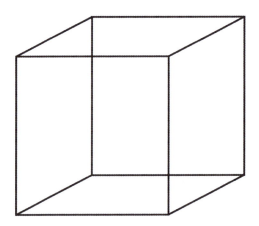

This ambiguous figure is called a Necker cube. If you keep looking at it for some time, you will find that it flips between two equally possible interpretations, as though the two views are competing for consciousness. But is this the right way of thinking about what is happening?

processing. The results showed that the activity of the cells in V1 stayed the same all the time, but the activity in the temporal cortex changed when the monkey's experience changed. More recent experiments with human subjects using brain-scanning techniques produced the same results.

Does this mean that the problem is solved and we have found where consciousness happens in the brain? Some researchers seem to think so. For example, Chalmers suggests that consciousness is generated in these areas, and the American neuropsychologist V. S. Ramachandran suggests that these brain cells are qualia-laden, while others are not. Similarly, Francis Crick (1916–2004), the Nobel Prize–winning physiologist, concludes that we are not conscious of the processing in early sensory areas but only of the later results of that processing.

Physiologist Francis Crick, codiscoverer with James D. Watson of the structure of the DNA molecule, is shown here with other 1962 laureates after the formal Nobel Prize ceremonies in Stockholm: (left to right) Professor Maurice H. Wilkins (medicine); Dr. Max Perutz (chemistry); Dr. Francis Crick (medicine); author John Steinbeck (literature); Professor James D. Watson (medicine); and Dr. John Kendrew (chemistry).

But the fundamental problem remains. We have no idea at all what it means to say that some computations are "qualia-laden," or that consciousness is "generated" in one brain area rather than another. When we have found the relevant brain cells, we must still ask—How? Why? What is the magic difference? How can some cells give rise to subjective experiences and some not?

It is certainly important to learn where these processes happen, but correlations alone do not solve the mystery. Indeed, they only make it more obvious that it is a mystery.

Damaged Minds

A stroke occurs when blood vessels in the brain become blocked, and the neurons deprived of oxygen are damaged. This frequently causes paralysis on the opposite side of the body, or blindness and other deficits on one side. This is easy to understand because the left brain controls the right side of the body, and the left brain sees the right side of the visual world (that is, the left brain deals not with the right eye, but with everything that is seen to the right of center). But a much odder effect can sometimes occur with right-brain damage: this is unilateral or hemifield neglect.

In this condition patients don't just lose some specific abilities; rather, they seem to lose half their world. It is not just that they cannot see when they look toward the left side of a room, or the left side of a picture, but rather that they seem not to realize that there even is a left side. This becomes obvious through their odd behavior. For example, they might eat only the food on the right side of their plate and completely ignore the rest until someone else turns the plate round. They might shave only the right side of their face, or respond only to visitors who stand on the right.

The Italian neurologist Edoardo Bisiach carried out a unique experiment on such patients. He asked them to imagine the famous cathedral square in Milan, which they all knew well. First, they had to describe what they would see if they were arriving at the Duomo from the north side. They all described the many beautiful buildings, shops, and cafés that they would see to their right. They completely ignored everything that would be to their left if they were standing in that position, and he could not get them to tell him what was there. But next he invited them to imagine coming into the square from the opposite side. Now all the forgotten buildings were carefully described and the previously remembered ones forgotten.

What is going on here? It is very difficult to accept that human experience could be fragmented like this. We like to imagine that surely if we had a stroke we would be able to recognize our silly mistake and brings the two views together, but clearly this just does not happen. For these people, half the world is simply gone and there is no higher conscious self who can overcome the problem.

Memory is also something we can easily take for granted until we consider the effects of losing it. There are two main types of memory, short- and long-term, but this major distinction can hide the many varied and subtle kinds of memory associated with specific tasks and abilities. This is important in older people whose memory for events is fading but who may still come to recognize places and routines, and learn new motor skills. Also, small areas of brain damage can affect very specific kinds of memory. Nonetheless, the most dramatic loss, and the most interesting for thinking about consciousness, is anterograde amnesia.

Anterograde amnesia usually occurs when the hippocampus (part of the brain's limbic system) is damaged, whether this is from Korsakoff's syndrome caused by alcohol poisoning, from surgery or illness, or from accidents that deprive the brain of oxygen. The result is that the person retains his or her short-term memory and the long-term memories he or she already has, but loses the capacity to lay down new long-term memories. So the rest of the person's life occurs as an ever-rolling present of a few seconds, which then disappears into blankness.

H. M. was one of the most famous cases of amnesia ever studied. He had both hippocampi removed in 1956 in a last-ditch attempt to control his severe epilepsy, and was left profoundly amnesic. He could learn some new skills and became quicker at recognizing certain stimuli, but he always denied ever having done the tasks before. C. W. was a musician who lost his memory through encephalitis. After the illness he could still enjoy music, sight-read, and even conduct his choir, but he could not remember the rehearsals or any other events that happened from then on.

Neurologist Oliver Sacks describes his experience with Jimmie G., a victim of Korsakoff's syndrome who, at the age of forty-nine, still believed he was nineteen and had just left the navy. Out of curiosity, Sacks showed Jimmie his own reflection in a mirror, but quickly regretted his action when Jimmie saw his own gray-haired face and became frantic with fear and incomprehension. So Sacks quickly led him over to the window where he noticed some kids playing outside. Jimmie's fear subsided, he began to smile, and Sacks stole away. When he returned Jimmie greeted him as though he were a complete stranger.

What is it like to be so deeply amnesic? Are H. M. and C. W. fully conscious? Are they conscious in a different way? Or what? If we could detect consciousness, measure it, or even define it properly, then we might get definite answers, but all we can do is observe people's behavior and listen to what they say. From observing them, one can see that they are

The tale of Jimmie G. is told in *The Man Who Mistook His Wife for a Hat* (1985), by physician and author Oliver Sacks, who is shown here in an undated photo.

obviously conscious in some senses; they are awake, alert, and interested in the world, and can describe how they feel. Yet in other ways their experience must be profoundly different.

In C. W.'s diary, he wrote the same words again and again: "I have just become conscious for the first time." Others exclaim, over and over, "I have just woken up." Perhaps we all know that vivid feeling of suddenly becoming acutely conscious, as though we had been dreaming or submerged in thought. This feeling of awakening may be triggered by the beauty of our surroundings, by a chance word or comment, or even by asking ourselves the question "Am I conscious now?" Whatever the cause, it can be a strange and special moment. But imagine living life as a perpetual awakening that you can never remember.

Such cases make us ponder the continuity of consciousness. While amnesics may experience the present as a unified stream of consciousness like anyone else's, and may even feel that their experience is continuous from moment to moment, they cannot have any sense of yesterday turning into today, or of planning for a future that connects to their past. If you believe in any kind of inner self, soul, or spirit, these facts are awkward to face. Is there a real self somewhere who is remembering everything but just cannot convey it to the damaged brain? Has the soul or self been damaged too, exactly in line with the physical damage to the brain? More likely is that our sense of a continuous conscious self is somehow manufactured by a fully functioning brain, but how?

These cases may help us think about how experience relates to brain function. Some even odder kinds of brain damage challenge the very idea of the unity of consciousness.

Seeing Without Seeing

D. F. is a patient with visual form agnosia. Even though her basic visual ability and her color vision are normal, she cannot recognize the forms or shapes of objects by sight, name simple line drawings, or recognize letters and digits. She can, however, reach out and grasp everyday objects with remarkable accuracy, even though she cannot say what they are.

In a fascinating experiment, D. F. was shown a series of slots—like a hole you might post a letter through—and asked to draw the orientation of the slot, or to adjust a line to the angle of the slot. She could not do this at all. However, when she was given a piece of card she could quickly line it up with the slot and post it through.

At first sight this might look as though D. F. is able to see (because she can post the cards) without having the *actual experience* of seeing; it would imply a dissociation between vision and consciousness, as though she were a visual zombie. This conclusion rests on our natural way of thinking about vision and consciousness, but research suggests that this conclusion is wrong.

The most natural way of thinking about vision is probably something like this: information comes into the eyes and is processed by the brain; this leads to our consciously seeing a picture of the world which we can then act upon. In other words, we must consciously see something before we can act on it. It turns out that the brain is not organized this way at all, and we could probably not survive if it were. In fact, there are (at least) two distinct visual streams with distinct functions.

The ventral stream leads from the primary visual cortex forward into the temporal cortex and is involved in building up accurate perceptions of the world. But these can take some time. So, in parallel with this, the dorsal stream leads into the parietal lobe and coordinates fast visuo-motor control. This means that fast visually guided actions, such as returning a serve, catching a ball, or jumping out of the way of an obstacle, can

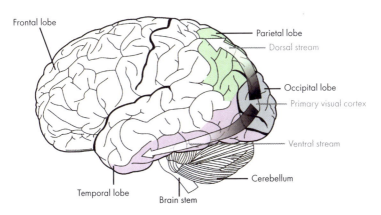

Two visual streams. The ventral stream is involved in perception and the dorsal stream in fast visuo-motor control.

happen long before you have recognized the ball or obstacle. D. F.'s case now makes sense. It is best described as a dissociation not between vision and consciousness, but between action and perception. She has lost much of the ventral stream that leads to visual perception but retains the dorsal stream needed for accurate visuo-motor control. Many other experiments have confirmed this general picture and suggest that our natural way of thinking about vision must be wrong.

In the 1970s, Oxford neuropsychologist Lawrence Weiskrantz made an even more extraordinary discovery. He was working with a patient called D. B., who had damage to the primary part of visual cortex called V1. This area has cells laid out in a map of the visual world, and so damage to it creates a blind area, or scotoma. That is, when the person looks steadily straight ahead, there is an area of the world in which they can see nothing at all. In normal life this may not matter too much because they can always move their eyes around, but in experiments it is easy to demonstrate that if you present them with an object or picture in the blind area, they say they cannot see it.

The odd discovery was this: Weiskrantz presented D. B. with a display of stripes at various different angles and asked him whether the stripes were vertical or horizontal. Naturally, D. B. said he had no idea because he could not see any stripes. But Weiskrantz made him guess. While still protesting that he was blind in that area, D. B. guessed—and he got the answer right nearly 90 percent of the time. In other words, he claimed to be blind, yet the data showed that he could see. Weiskrantz called this paradoxical condition "blindsight."

Many subsequent experiments have been done with other blindsight patients and with similar results. While denying consciously seeing anything, some can move their eyes toward objects, point to the location of objects, or mimic the movement of lights or objects in the blind field. Others show pupil dilation and other emotional responses to stimuli, and several can correctly guess the color of stimuli they say they cannot "see."

Blindsight looks, at first sight, to be a clincher for theories of consciousness. The argument might go like this: the blindseer has objective vision without subjective consciousness; he is a partial zombie who can see without having the qualia of seeing; this proves that consciousness is an added extra and is separate from the physical functions of vision; it proves that qualia exist and that functionalism and materialism are false.

But things are not so simple. The most likely explanation of blindsight depends on the fact that there are something like ten separate, parallel pathways along which visual information flows through the brain. About 85 percent of cells take the major route to primary visual cortex, but the rest go via other minor routes to other cortical and subcortical areas. These other pathways are not affected by the destruction of V1 that causes blindsight. So the odd abilities of the blindseer probably depend on using these other pathways. As an example, suppose that a pathway that controls eye movements remains intact. Then it is not surprising that the patient's eyes move to track an object in the blind field. He may even feel his own eyes moving and so be able to guess that there is an object there. But without V1 he cannot possibly recognize the object or detect its shape, size, or other features. In this sense he really is blind.

If this is the right interpretation, blindsight remains a fascinating phenomenon, but it does not prove that consciousness can be separated from the processes of vision. If it tells us anything about consciousness, it is that our ordinary concept of a single central visual experience is probably completely wrong. And how any visual experience comes to be conscious remains as far from explanation as ever.

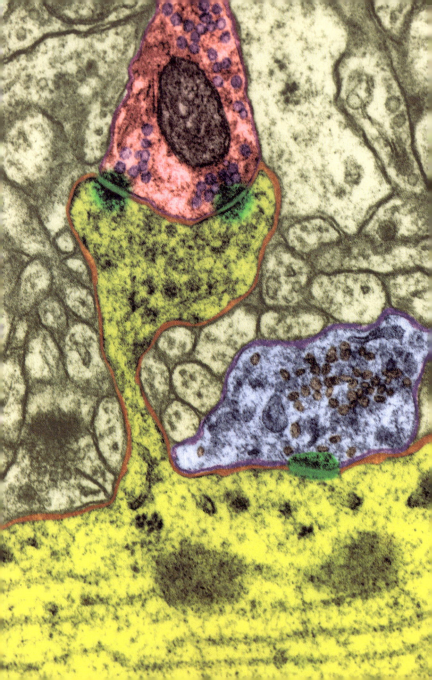

THREE

Time and Space

•

The Timing of Experience

Could consciousness lag behind the events of the real world? This curious question emerged from research begun in the 1960s by neuroscientist Benjamin Libet. His findings have led to theories about "Libet's delay" or the "half-second lag" and, as we shall see in Chapter 6, to implications for free will and responsibility.

The earliest of Libet's experiments were performed on patients who had had the surface of their brains exposed for necessary surgery, and

After a touch on the skin a signal travels up the spinal cord, through the brain stem and the thalamus, to the sensory cortex. On the way it crosses many synapses (the gaps between adjacent neurons), like the excitatory synapse shown here on a dendritic spine at a magnification of ×8,180. From skin to cortex takes about one-hundredth of a second. But what happens then? When do "I" become conscious of the touch? Experiments with brain stimulation show a curious delay of half a second.

they gave their permission for Libet to stimulate the brain surface with electrodes. It had long been known that the part of the brain called somatosensory cortex contains a map of the body and that stimulating any part of it causes a sensation as though the corresponding part of the body is being touched. If motor cortex is stimulated, a part of the body moves; if visual cortex is stimulated, things are seen, and so on.

Libet used trains of electrical stimulation varying in length from a few milliseconds (thousandths of a second) to over a second, and what he found was this: with short trains of electrical pulses the patients felt nothing, but with longer bursts they said they could feel something like a touch on their arms. Libet showed that it needed half a second of continuous electrical stimulation for the patient to say "I feel it." It seemed as though the conscious experience came a full half second after the stimulation began.

Confirmation of this odd finding came from experiments using a technique for blocking, or masking, conscious sensations. It was already known that stimulating somatosensory cortex just after a real touch on the arm prevents the touch being felt, so Libet varied the timing. If he stimulated the brain more than half a second after the touch, then the patient still felt the touch, but if he did it before the half second had passed, then the sensation of touch was obliterated as though it had never been.

The most obvious interpretation (though not necessarily the correct one) was that it takes half a second of neuronal activity to produce consciousness. Libet called this "neuronal adequacy for consciousness." This is very odd. It implies that consciousness must lag far behind the events of the real world and so must be useless in responding to a fast-moving world. It is important here to realize how long half a second is in brain terms. The signal from a real touch on the arm reaches the brain in a few hundredths of a second, and sounds get there even faster. The typical reaction time to a flash of light is about a fifth of a second, and that involves many neurons being activated to detect the light and then coordinate the response. It seems crazy that consciousness could come so late in the proceedings, but this is what Libet's results seemed to show.

If this is true, why don't we realize it? Libet's own explanation involves the phenomenon of "backward referral" or "subjective antedating." He argues that consciousness does indeed require half a second of continuous activity in the cortex, but that we do not notice the delay because the events are referred back in time once neuronal adequacy has been reached. This is possible because when a stimulus happens—say, a flash of light or a quick touch—there is an immediate effect in the brain called the "evoked potential." According to Libet's theory, when we consciously feel a touch on the arm, activity builds up in the somatosensory cortex until neuronal adequacy is reached. Once it is reached, then the apparent timing of the touch is referred back to the time of the evoked potential. Otherwise nothing is felt. In this way no delay in consciousness is ever noticed.

Libet's experiments are unlikely ever to be repeated because advances in medicine have made that kind of invasive surgery unnecessary. However, they are usually accepted as valid by most researchers in the field. What is not agreed is the correct interpretation. Libet himself is among those antimaterialists who believe the results challenge the equivalence of mind and brain. Dualists such as the philosopher of science Sir Karl Popper (1902–94) and neurophysiologist Sir John Eccles (1903–97) take the results as evidence for the power of the nonphysical mind, and mathematician Sir Roger Penrose claims that quantum theory is required to explain them.

Churchland and Dennett completely disagree. They argue that the results only appear to have these peculiar implications because people will not give up their false idea of consciousness, and remain stuck in the Cartesian theater. This makes the problem of consciousness seem insoluble when it should not be.

This objection is worth exploring a little more deeply. The natural way to think about the half-second delay is probably something like this. A touch on the arm (or any other stimulus) causes signals to pass along the nerves of the arm, and into the brain, where the information is processed in the relevant areas until it finally arrives in consciousness and the person feels the touch. In this view, there are two different kinds of phenomenon, each with its own timing. First, there are objective events with physical times that can be measured with instruments, such as the time of the electrical stimulus or the time at which a given brain cell fires. Then there are subjective experiences with their own times, such as the time at which the experience of the touch happens, or when the touch comes into consciousness.

This description may seem quite unexceptionable. Indeed, you may be convinced that it has to be correct. But note all the trouble it leads us into. If you accept this apparently obvious way of thinking about the brain, then you are stuck either with a place in the brain where physical events correspond to mental ones, or with a time at which unconscious processes magically turn into conscious ones: the time at which they "become conscious" or "enter consciousness." But what on earth could this mean? Thinking this way, you hit right up against the hard problem and the apparently insoluble mystery of consciousness.

One way forward is to stick with this natural view of consciousness and try to solve the problem, explaining how unconscious processes turn into conscious ones. This is the approach that leads to quantum theory, various kinds of dualism, and, indeed, most scientific theories of consciousness that we have. Libet's own suggestion is that when physical activity in a group of brain cells has been going on long enough it turns from being unconscious one moment to being conscious the next, but he does not explain how or why, and the mystery remains.

A much more radical alternative is to throw out the assumption that conscious experiences can be timed. Giving up the natural view of consciousness is extremely difficult, but some other odd examples may make the possibility more attractive.

Clocks and Rabbits

Imagine that you are sitting reading a book when, just as you turn the page, you realize that the clock is chiming. A moment ago you were not aware of the chimes but now, suddenly, the noise has entered your awareness. At that moment, you can remember the sounds you were not listening to and count the chimes you did not hear. There have been three already and you go on listening until you find that it is six o'clock.

This is a particularly powerful example because you can check that you counted correctly, but a similar thing happens all the time with background noises. You may suddenly become aware of that drilling noise out in the road. Until that moment you were not aware of it, but now it seems as though you can remember what it sounded like before you became aware of it. It seems almost as though someone, if not you, had been listening all along. These experiences are so familiar that we tend to ignore them, but they are worth thinking about a little more carefully.

Take the example of the clock. If the ordinary view of consciousness is correct, then we should be able to say which experiences were in the theater or stream of consciousness, and which were not. So what about the first three "dongs" of the clock? If you say that they were in the stream (i.e., conscious) all along, then you cannot explain the very definite impression that you only became conscious of them later. On the other hand, if you say that they were outside the stream (unconscious), then you have to explain what happened when you became conscious of them. Were they unconscious until the fourth dong and then subjectively referred back in time, as Libet might say? Were memories of them held in some unconscious state only to be switched to being conscious when your attention switched? Quite apart from the difficulty of explaining what this switch could mean, this leaves us with a rather odd kind of stream because it now contains a mixture of things that we were conscious of all along, and ones that only got pulled in retrospectively.

Many other examples reveal the same peculiarity. In a noisy room full of people talking, you may suddenly switch your attention because someone behind you has said "Guess what Jeremy was saying yesterday about Sue . . . she . . ." You prick up your ears. At this point you seem to have been aware of the whole sentence as it was spoken. But were you really? The fact is that you would never have noticed it at all if your name had not been mentioned. So was the sentence in or out of the stream?

In fact, this problem really applies to all of speech. You need to accumulate a lot of serial information before the beginning of the sentence becomes comprehensible. What was in the stream of consciousness while all this was happening? Was it just meaningless noises or gobbledygook? Did it switch from gobbledygook to words halfway through? It doesn't feel like that. It feels as though you listened and heard a meaningful sentence as it went along, but this is impossible. Or take just one word, or listen to a robin singing. Only once the song is complete, or the word finished, can you know what it was that you heard. What was in the stream of consciousness before this point?

An ingenious experiment, called the "cutaneous rabbit," demonstrates the problem at its most obvious. To get this effect a person holds out his or her arm and looks the other way while the experimenter taps the person's arm. In the original experiment a tapping machine was used, but the effect can be demonstrated using carefully practiced taps with a sharp pencil. The critical point is to tap at precisely equal intervals and with equal pressure, five times at the wrist, three times near the elbow, and twice near the shoulder.

What does the person feel? Oddly enough, the person feels a series of taps running rapidly from wrist to shoulder, not in three distinct bursts,

but as though a little rabbit were scampering all the way up his or her arm—hence the "cutaneous rabbit."

The effect is odd and makes people laugh, but the questions it poses are serious ones. How does the brain know where to put the second, third, and fourth taps when the tap on the elbow has not yet occurred? If you stick to the natural idea that any tap (say, the fourth one) must have been either conscious or unconscious (in the stream or out of it), then you get into a big muddle. For example, you might have to say that the third tap was consciously experienced at its correct place, that is, on the wrist, but then later, after the sixth tap occurred, this memory was wiped out and replaced with the conscious experience of it happening halfway between wrist and elbow. If you don't like this idea, you might prefer to say that consciousness was held up for some time—waiting for all the taps to come in before deciding where to place each one. In this case, the fourth tap remained unconscious until after the sixth tap occurred, and was then referred back in time so as to be put in its correct place in the stream of consciousness.

Once again, we seem to be faced with an unpleasant choice; either deal with these problems or abandon the natural idea of the stream of conscious experiences. One last example may reveal yet more trouble in the stream.

Driving Unconsciously

What is attention? In 1890, William James famously proclaimed that "every one knows what attention is," but many subsequent arguments and thousands of experiments later it seems that no one knows what attention is, and there may not even be a single process to study. Attention is one of those aspects of consciousness that seems obvious and easy to understand at first sight but gets more peculiar the more you think about it.

The most natural way to think about attention is as a spotlight that we can shine on some things while leaving others in the dark. Sometimes this spotlight is grabbed against our will by a loud noise or someone calling our name, but at other times we direct the spotlight ourselves, choosing now to think about the book we are reading and then to look out of the window for a minute or two. This power to direct attention not only is something we value, but seems to be something that our consciousness does. It *seems* as though I consciously decide what to attend to, but do I really?

If we think about what is going on inside the brain, this natural idea becomes much harder to understand. Inside the brain there are numerous processes going on in parallel, coordinating perceptions and thoughts, and controlling our behavior. Perhaps the best way to think about attention is as a system, or collection of systems, for allocating the brain's resources. So when I am concentrating on a conversation, there is more processing capacity given over to the auditory and language parts of my brain than to vision and touch; when my attention is on watching a game, there is more given over to vision, and so on.

Now we may ask what directs this allocation of resources? Psychologists have done thousands of experiments showing how different stimuli can direct attention, how attention can be divided, and which parts of the brain are active when this happens. But where, then, is the role for consciousness? What could correspond in brain terms to the powerful sense that I am in there consciously directing the show? This is just one of many reasons why the relationship between consciousness and attention is not obvious. Even though great progress has been made in understanding attention, there is no generally agreed theory that relates it to consciousness. While some theorists equate consciousness and attention, others claim they are completely different phenomena. Some claim that there can be no consciousness without attention, and others disagree.

The unconscious driving phenomenon vividly illustrates this problem. Anyone who has become a proficient driver has probably had this peculiar experience. You set off on a familiar journey to work, or school, or a friend's house, and as you drive you start thinking about something else. In no time at all you have arrived. You know you must have driven all that way but you can remember nothing of the drive at all. It is as though you were completely unconscious of the whole process, even though you were wide-awake.

What is going on here? One suggestion is that you were attending to your daydreams instead of your driving. But if attention is conceived of as a matter of processing resources, then this cannot be true. Driving is not a simple task, and a lot of processing resources must have been allocated to it. On that journey you probably stopped at several red lights and set off again when they turned green, negotiated intersections, kept a safe distance from the car in front, adjusted your speed to compensate for hills and bends, slowed down when you saw a speed limit sign, and waved to thank someone who let you pull out. These are all skilled tasks; they require complex coordination of vision, hearing, motor control, decision making, and more. So the important point is not that your brain wasn't paying any attention to the task, but that it was doing it automatically and you were not *conscious* of it. It is as though all of that activity was going on without you.

How can we make sense of this? It seems easy and natural to invoke the usual metaphors of the theater or stream to describe the difference. In the conscious case, all those changing traffic lights, hills, bends, and other cars were on show in our mental theater and were experienced in our stream of consciousness; in the unconscious case, the daydreams took over the show, and the lights and bends and cars never made it into the stream of consciousness.

The problem only appears when we try to relate this idea to what is going on in the brain. Let's consider the brain processes involved in one small aspect of driving, for example, observing the light change to red and stopping the car. In both the conscious and unconscious cases, a great deal of processing must have gone on in visual cortex, in the planning parts of frontal cortex, and in motor cortex, where the movements of hands and feet are coordinated. In both cases, you successfully stopped the car, and yet in one case all this activity was conscious and in the other it was not. What is the difference?

As we have seen, there is no central screen in the brain where a self watches the show, no central processor where the conscious bits happen, and yet there must be some important difference. What is it? This is what any viable theory of consciousness has to explain. It is time to consider some of the most popular theories and learn how they cope with this magic difference.

Theories of Consciousness

I get lots of letters and e-mails from people who claim to have solved the mystery of consciousness and want to tell me their theory. The vast majority fall into two categories: either they are dualist theories that propose a separate mind, soul, or spirit, or they invoke the wonders of modern physics.

Dualism (the idea that mind and body are separate) is always tempting because it fits so well with the way our consciousness feels, but there are very few philosophers or scientists who think it could be true. Almost the only modern example is the dualist interactionism proposed by Popper and Eccles in the 1970s. They argued for a non-physical, self-conscious mind that is separate from the unconscious physical brain. This mind is able to influence its brain through finely balanced interactions taking place at the billions of synapses (junctions between neurons). Popper and Eccles can easily explain unconscious driving by saying that the nonphysical mind was engaging only with the daydreaming parts of the brain, not with the vision and driving parts. However, in common with other kinds of dualism, this provides no explanation for how subjective experience comes about (it is just posited as a property of the self-conscious mind) and no explanation of how the interaction works.

All the attempts at dualist theories that I have come across face similar problems. The separate mind is invented to do the job of being conscious, but there is no satisfactory explanation of how it interacts with the world or the brain—other than by magic.

Theories based in modern physics take a different approach. Some liken the nonlocality and peculiar behavior of time found in quantum physics to similar effects in consciousness; others draw upon the controversial idea that a conscious observer is required to explain the collapse of the wave function in quantum mechanics; but the best known is based on quantum computing in microtubules. Anaesthetist Stuart Hameroff and mathematician Sir Roger Penrose argue that the tiny microtubules found in every brain cell are not the simple structural elements they are usually

Popper and Eccles proposed the existence of a nonphysical, self-conscious mind that is separate from but can influence the unconscious physical brain through interactions that take place at the synapses, or junctions between neurons, though they did not explain how this could possibly work. Austrian philosopher Karl Popper (1902–94) is shown here in a photograph taken on August 31, 1992.

thought to be, but are designed to allow for quantum coherence and brain-wide quantum connections. This, they claim, explains the unity of consciousness and the possibility of free will, as well as Libet's odd timing effects. The real difficulty here lies with subjectivity. Even if quantum computing does occur in brains (which is highly controversial), this still does not explain how private subjective experiences can emerge. Many people conclude that quantum theories of consciousness do no more than replace one mystery with another.

All the other theories I will discuss are based on conventional philosophy and neuroscience, such as the "higher-order thought" (HOT) theories in philosophy. These suggest that sensations and thoughts are conscious only if the person also has a higher-order thought to the effect that they are conscious of them. So, for example, the driver's perception of the red light would be conscious only if accompanied by a HOT that he or she is seeing a red light. HOT theories account for the magic difference without invoking any special consciousness neurons; conscious thoughts are those that have HOTs about them. They also deal easily with some of the odd timing effects because HOTs take time to build up, but they deny consciousness to other animals that cannot have HOTs, and cannot account for such states as deep meditation in which people claim to be very conscious without any thoughts at all. As for the unconscious driving phenomenon, this is explained only if we suppose that all along the person was thinking "I am now daydreaming."

More firmly rooted in psychology and neuroscience is global workspace theory, first proposed by psychologist Bernard Baars in the 1980s. This starts from the idea that the brain is functionally organized around a global workspace, in which just a few items at a time can be processed, and depends heavily on the theater metaphor. The very few items that are in consciousness at any time correspond to those in the bright spot on the center of the stage, lit up by the spotlight of attention, and surrounded by a less conscious fringe. Beyond the stage is an unconscious audience sitting in the dark with numerous unconscious contextual systems that shape the events happening on the stage.

In this theory what makes an event conscious is that it is being processed within the global workspace and is therefore broadcast to the rest of the (unconscious) system. So when you are driving consciously, the information about red lights and other cars is processed in the global workspace and is broadcast to the rest of the brain. This makes it available to influence other behaviors such as speech and memory. When your workspace is filled with daydreams, the lights and cars are relegated to the fringe, or even to the darkness, and are not broadcast.

According to one theory, when you are driving consciously, the red lights and other cars around you are processed in the brain's global workspace and broadcast to the rest of the brain. Other theories claim that the difference between conscious and unconscious driving is only whether you remember it afterward or not.

The advantage of this theory is that it states clearly which things should be

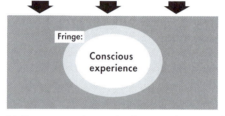

Context operators behind the scenes

Director	Spotlight Controller	Local Contexts

Competing for access to consciousness:

the players...

Outer Senses	**Inner Senses**	**Ideas**
Seeing		
Hearing	Visual Imagery	Imaginable Ideas
Feeling	Inner Speech	Verbalized Ideas
Tasting	Dreams	Fringe Conscious
Smelling	Imagined	Institutions
Submodalities	Feelings	
Heat		
Vibration		

the spotlight of attention shining on the stage of working memory...

Fringe:

Conscious experience

Working memory receives conscious input, controls inner speech, uses imagery for spatial tasks, all under voluntary control.

the unconscious audience ...

Memory systems:

Lexicon
Semantic networks
Autobiographical & declarative memory
Beliefs, knowledge of the world, of oneself and others.

Interpreting conscious contents:

Recognizing objects, faces, speech, events. Syntactic analysis. Spatial relationships. Social inferences.

Automatisms:

Skill memory. Details of language, action control, reading, thinking, and thousands more ...

Motivational systems:

Is the conscious event relevant to my goals? Emotional responses, facial expressions, preparing the body for action. Managing goal conflicts.

Global workspace theory. According to Baars, the contents of consciousness are the contents of the brain's global workspace, corresponding to the brightly lit stage in the theater of the mind. (From B. Baars, In the theatre of consciousness, *Journal of Consciousness Studies*, 4, no. 4 (1997): 29–309, p. 300. Reproduced with permission.)

conscious, that is, those that are in the workspace and are globally available. The difficulty with this theory is to explain why information that is broadcast, or made globally available to an unconscious audience, should thereby be conscious (i.e., experienced) while other information is not. In fact, the central problem of subjectivity remains as mysterious as ever.

This is probably true of most of the theories we have. For example, neurobiologists Gerald Edelman and Giulio Tononi propose that consciousness emerges when large neuronal groups form a dynamic core in the brain, with connections looping back and forth between the thalamus and cortex. Pharmacologist Susan Greenfield suggests that consciousness is not an all-or-nothing phenomenon but increases with the size of neural assemblies, or large groups of interconnected neurons that work together. This may be so, but these theories do not explain why any neural network, however large or appropriately organized, should give rise to subjective experiences in the first place.

They may ultimately do so, and it is a perfectly sound strategy to try to propose neural structures that might be implicated in consciousness and then try to find out how they work. Edelman and Tononi are attempting this in terms of how the properties of neuronal groups relate to the properties of consciousness. In the end, this strategy may well pay off, but so far I would say that no theory can solve the basic mystery of subjective experience. All these theories accept the basic premise that at any time a small number of things are "in" the theater or stream of consciousness while all the rest are not, but they fail to explain how any kind of objective brain activity can give rise to a stream of conscious experiences.

· · · · ·

WHAT ARE YOU CONSCIOUS OF NOW?

You may be sure that you know exactly what is in your consciousness now, but do you? For many years I have encouraged my students to ask themselves a series of increasingly difficult questions hundreds of times a day, such as "Am I conscious now?," "Who is conscious now?," or "Did I do that consciously?" Typically, they go from being sure that they are conscious all day, to having serious doubts. They realize that asking the question makes a difference.

"What was I conscious of a moment ago?" is particularly interesting, and I have devoted many hours' meditation to it. If there really is a stream of consciousness, then there should be one answer—I was conscious of this not that. But once you start seriously looking, you find that you can look back and pick up any of several different threads— such as the noise of the traffic, the feeling of breathing, or the look of the grass. At first, picking one seems to chase away the others, but with practice consciousness changes. It becomes clear that there are always lots of threads going on at once, and none is really "in" consciousness until it is grasped.

Could exploring consciousness change consciousness itself? If so, we might easily be deluded, or learn to throw off the delusion.

· · · · ·

A completely different approach is to give up trying to explain the theater of consciousness—not by becoming a mysterian and saying that we feeble humans can never understand such a great mystery, but instead by claiming that the theater is an illusion. As we have seen, Dennett claimed that the Cartesian theater does not exist. In his theory of multiple drafts he goes even further and throws out altogether the idea that the mind is like a theater, or even that some things are in our consciousness while others are not. According to Dennett the brain processes multiple parallel descriptions of the world all the time, and none of them is either "in" or "out" of consciousness. When the system is probed in a certain way—say, by asking someone what he or she is conscious of, or getting the person to respond to a stimulus—then the person may decide what he or she is conscious of and tell you about it. But up to that point there was no truth of the matter about whether that thing was, or was not, "in consciousness."

This theory is deeply counterintuitive; it rejects our conviction that we all know exactly what we are conscious of—or which qualia we are experiencing—at any time. But it has the advantage of coping very well with the peculiar timing effects we have met here. Libet's delay occurs because it takes time for information to become available to a verbal probe. The chimes of the clock, and the driving, were never either in or out of consciousness, so the problems do not arise. But doesn't this do away with the very phenomenon we are trying to explain? Some people think it does and accuse Dennett of "explaining away" consciousness.

I disagree. There is obviously something we call "consciousness" that demands explanation. But is it really the unified stream of experiences we think it is? I suspect that we may have to give up the idea that each of us knows what is in our consciousness now, and accept that we might be deeply deluded about our own minds.

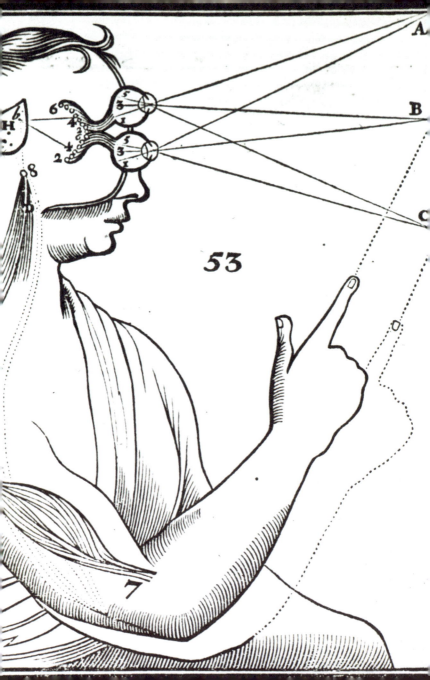

FOUR

A Grand Illusion

•

The Nature of Illusion

Is consciousness an illusion? The possibility that we might be seriously wrong about our own minds pops up in many guises—that free will is an illusion, that the Cartesian theater is an illusion, that self is an illusion, and that the richness of our visual world is a "grand illusion."

We should first be clear about this word *illusion*. The dictionary defines it as:

> The fact or condition of being deceived or deluded by appearances
> . . . a false conception or idea; a deception, delusion, fancy. (OED)

Beliefs about how vision and perception work, and how they relate to consciousness, are still a subject of debate, but it seems clear that how we think we see and how we really see are two very different things. This illustration by René Descartes showing a theory of vision was published in Descartes's *Treatise on Man* (1686). He understood how the lens forms an image on the back of the eye but could not understand what happens next.

or

> Perception of something objectively existing in such a way as to cause misinterpretation of its actual nature. (Webster)

In other words, an illusion is not something that does not exist but something that is not the way it seems.

Most familiar are visual illusions like that on page 63. This was named the "Cafe Wall Illusion" by British psychologist Richard Gregory, who investigated the extraordinary effect of this pattern after seeing it on the front wall of a café in Bristol. Numerous experiments have revealed how and why processing in the retina and visual cortex leads to the false conclusion that the tiles are not square and the lines of mortar are tilted. This disturbing illusion is most effective when the gray of the mortar is midway between the black and the white of the tiles, and the tiles offset by half a tile width. As with so many visual illusions, we can cover up parts of the image and prove to ourselves that the lines really are parallel and the squares, square, but this does not destroy the illusion.

Could something similar apply to the whole of consciousness? The claim then is not that consciousness does not exist, but that it is not what it seems to be. This means that our natural ideas about the way consciousness seems must be wrong and we should throw them out. Since we seem to get into such trouble when trying to understand consciousness, this idea might help.

To pursue this idea, we must start from the way consciousness seems and then consider why this might be wrong. One powerful temptation is to think of the mind as a theater (we have already considered why this might be false). Another is the impression that consciousness is some

An illusion is something that is not what it seems. In the café wall illusion the horizontal lines appear to be slanted. You may work out that they are really parallel, and intellectually believe it, but you cannot stop seeing them as slanted.

kind of force or power, and that we need it for the cleverest or most difficult things we do. Good examples might be creative thinking, decision making, and problem solving, but in fact it turns out that some of these can best be done unconsciously.

Here is a simple example: a children's riddle.

One sunny day I was walking across a field when I came upon an old scarf, a carrot, and two pieces of coal lying in the grass. How did they get there?

If you cannot solve this one straightaway, you should have a go struggling with it; think all around it, try to work out the answer consciously, conjure up a really vivid image of the scene, and do your best. The answer really is obvious once you get it. If you still cannot see it, then just let the problem "incubate" and see what happens. (The answer is on page 81 but don't look now.)

Studies of incubation show that when people first work on a problem and then drop it to think about something else, the answer sometimes just pops up with no conscious effort at all. Something similar happens with creative artists and scientists. Brilliant innovations and solutions to scientific problems do not just appear by magic; what usually happens is that the scientist or inventor struggles for hours, days, or even years with a difficult problem, putting all the pieces together, working out the difficulties but failing to find a solution. Then they stop struggling, think about something else, and find that all of a sudden, "pop" the solution appears—a eureka moment! It is as though some part of the mind has been working away and found the solution on its own.

Experiments have also explored special problems that are too complex to solve by logical thinking, yet can be solved. They require something else; something we might call intuition. In a famous study people played a computer game that simulated sugar production in a factory. They could control variables such as the number of workers and their pay, but had no idea of the equations that ran the simulation. Very quickly they got better at stabilizing sugar production, but they had no idea how they did it. In fact, those who thought they knew what they were doing often performed worse at the task than those who did not.

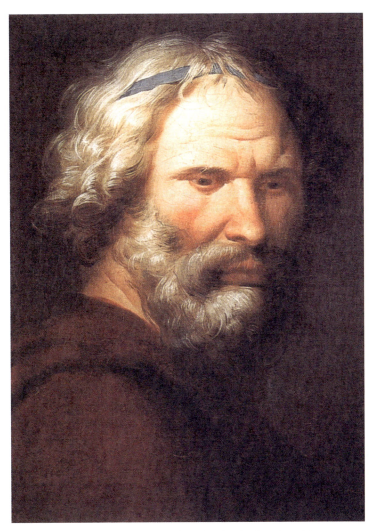

The common use of *eureka* is most famously attributed to Greek mathematician Archimedes (ca. 287–212 BCE), who is shown here in a portrait by Sicilian artist Giuseppe Patania (1780–1852).

Something similar is probably going on all the time in our highly complex social worlds. We meet someone new, see the person's face, clothes, and gestures, hear the person's voice, and quickly judge him or her as friendly or cold, trustworthy or dubious, intelligent or not, but how? Along with all our innate abilities, we have a lifetime's history of meeting people and seeing how they turned out. We could not possibly remember all this explicitly, or work out the equations that give the probabilities involved, but somewhere in the system all this is being done and so we end up making reliable judgments.

This kind of implicit processing explains much of what we call emotional decision making, or intuition, for we do not know where the answers come from—we just seem to feel what is right or "know" what we should do. These are important skills that are often overlooked. Historically, many thinkers have admired rationality at the expense of the emotions, elevating purely rational thought above everything else, and separating the rational mind from the body. This is what neuroscientist Antonio Damasio calls "Descartes' Error." He provides evidence that the ability to feel emotions is intrinsic to thinking and decision making. For example, people with frontal lobe damage become emotionally flat, yet rather than become super-rational decision makers, they seem unable to make up their minds at all.

We can also respond to all sorts of stimuli of which we are not consciously aware, that is, to subliminal (or under-the-threshold) stimuli. Subliminal perception has had a bad reputation, perhaps because of claims that advertisers could make people buy their products by inserting very brief messages into films or television programs. In fact, this kind of trick does not work, and people's buying behavior is hardly affected. Nor do subliminal tapes work. For example, there are claims that listening to a tape with inaudible messages on, or playing it while you sleep, will teach you new languages or new skills, or change your life. In fact, unless you can hear the messages you will learn next to nothing.

These claims aside, subliminal perception is a real phenomenon. For example, when people are primed with a word flashed too briefly to see it consciously, the word can still affect their reactions. So if *river* is flashed and not seen, the next word *bank* is more likely to be interpreted as a riverbank than a place to keep money. Similarly, if smiling or frowning faces are flashed, people are more likely to respond positively or negatively, respectively, to meaningless symbols shown straight afterward. These and many other experiments imply that all the time we are affected by countless unnoticed events going on around us. Our clever brains process all this information in fantastically complex ways, and yet we consciously know little about it.

The temptation is to imagine something like this: the human mind consists of a vast unconscious part, some smaller preconscious or subconscious parts, and finally the conscious mind, which is what we know about and experience directly. But I think this traditional image has to be wrong.

Filling in the Gaps

Have you ever had the experience of suddenly seeing something right in front of your eyes that you had not noticed before—those glasses you thought you'd lost; a book you hadn't noticed; a snowman in the neighbor's garden? What was in your consciousness before that moment? As William James exclaimed in 1890, "There would have been *gaps*—but we felt no gaps." There were no glasses or book-shaped gaps in our picture of the room, no snowman-shaped empty space on the lawn. Had our mind filled in over the gap? Did it need to?

This common experience seems odd, but the reason it seems odd is probably something like this. We imagine that somewhere inside our head or mind there is a complete picture of the world, which is our conscious experience. After all, when we look around we see a world with no gaps, so we assume that there must be such a gap-free world represented inside. This idea of an inner, detailed representation in the head has been the underlying assumption of most of cognitive science for many decades. Yet it may be wrong to think of our minds this way, as some simple experiments can show.

First, there is the blind spot. The human eye is designed in a most curious way, which, incidentally, reveals the haphazard way in which evolution works. Somewhere in our ancestors' far past, simple eyes developed in which the neurons carrying the information from the few light-receptor cells went forward before going back to the simple brain. Natural selection always works on whatever it has to hand, and so this primitive eye was modified and gradually developed into a complex eye with muscles, lenses, and thousands of receptors tightly packed together. By this time the neurons were getting in the way of the light, but evolution cannot, as it were, decide it has taken a wrong path and go back and start again. So the original plan stayed. The consequence is that we have neurons obscuring our receptors and then coming together into a big bundle called the optic nerve, which goes out through the retina, making a hole (about fifteen degrees out from the center) in which there are no receptors at all. In this part of the eye we are totally blind. Do we notice? Not at all. To demonstrate this to yourself, try the test on the top of page 69.

In ordinary life we simply do not notice these two blind spots. Part of the reason is that we have two eyes, so each compensates for the other,

Finding the blind spot: Hold the book out at arm's length. Put a hand over your right eye and look at the small black dot with your left eye. Now move the page toward you slowly. At some distance you will find that the star disappears. This is because it is now falling on your blind spot.

but even when we cover one eye we do not see a hole in our vision. Why not? It is the same question as before. Does the brain fill in the missing bits to cover over the gap? And if so, with what? There have been heated debates about this question of filling-in.

Dennett argues that the brain does not need to fill in the gaps with details and does not do so. This is because seeing is not a process of building up a picture-like copy of the world for an inner self to look at, but is more like making guesses or assumptions about what is there. This kind of conceptual filling-in happens all the time. Right now you can probably see many objects obscuring others: a book covering up part of the desk, the carpet disappearing behind a table leg, scenery obscured by a car. Of course you don't see a car-shaped hole in the scenery—but nor do you need to fill in the missing piece with plausible trees and bushes. Your visual experience is that there is continuous scenery even though you cannot see all of it.

Dennett now asks us to imagine walking into a room papered all over with identical portraits of Marilyn Monroe. We would, he says, see within a few seconds that there were hundreds of identical portraits, and would quickly notice if one had a hat or a silly mustache. Our natural conclusion is that we must now have a detailed picture of all those Marilyns in our head. But, says Dennett, this cannot be so. Only the fovea, in the center of our retina, sees clearly, and our eyes make only about four or five saccades (large eye movements) each second, so we could not possibly have looked clearly at each portrait. Our ability to see so much depends on texture detectors that can see a repeating pattern across the whole room, and dedicated pop-out mechanisms that would draw attention to oddities like a silly mustache or a different color. So what we see is not a detailed inner picture at all but something more like a guess, or hypothesis, or representation that there are lots of identical portraits. The brain does not need to represent each Marilyn individually in an inner picture, and does not do so. We get the vivid impression that all that detail is inside our heads, but really it remains out there in the world. There is no need to fill in the missing Marilyns and the brain does not do so.

But filling-in really does happen, according to psychologists Richard Gregory and V. S. Ramachandran. They created artificial blind spots by asking people to look straight at the center of a display of flickering "snow." Offset by six degrees was a small gray square with no snow. At first the subjects saw the square, but after about five seconds it became filled with snow like the rest of the screen. Next, when the whole screen was made gray, a square of snow appeared and lasted for two or three seconds. Other experiments revealed separate mechanisms for filling in color, texture, and movement. For example, in one, the background was sparse twinkling black dots on a pink background, and the square was black spots moving horizontally on gray. In a few seconds the square faded, but it did so in two distinct stages. First the gray changed to pink, and then the moving dots changed to twinkling ones.

Another similar experiment used a background of English or Latin text. The square was filled in as before, but curiously the subjects now said that they could see that there were letters in the square but could not read them. Interestingly, this effect is also found in dreams in which people find books, newspapers, or enormous signs and can see the writing but cannot read it. So what are they seeing? Perhaps it is more like the *idea* of writing than an area covered with actual letters.

The debates about filling-in are far from over, but these experiments suggest that filling-in does occur but is not like completing the details dot by dot in an inner picture.

Blindness to Change

Imagine you are the subject in an experiment and you are asked to look at the picture on page 72. Then, at precisely the moment that you move your eyes, the picture is changed to the one on page 73. Would you notice the difference? Most people are sure that they would. But they are wrong.

This is the phenomenon of change blindness and has been demonstrated in many different ways. The first experiments, in the 1980s, used eye trackers. A laser beam, reflected off the subject's eye, detected eye movements and instantly changed the text or picture that the subject was looking at. Subjects failed to notice even large and apparently obvious changes. Eye trackers are expensive, but I tried the simpler method of forcing people to move their eyes by moving the picture slightly and changing it at the same time. I found the same effect and concluded that the richness of our visual world is an illusion.

Change blindness. If these two pictures were swapped just as you moved your eyes or blinked, you would not see the change. Experiments on change blindness suggest that seeing does not entail building up a detailed representation of the visual world.

Subsequently many other methods have been used. The easiest is to have a brief gray flash between the two pictures; the pictures can then be flicked back and forth, from one to the other, until the observer sees the change. Typically, it can take people many minutes to detect even a large object that changes color, or one that disappears altogether. This is a most frustrating experience. You look and look and see nothing changing; if you are with other people you hear them laughing; then suddenly you see the obvious and cannot imagine how you could have missed it.

The effect works because all these methods inactivate the pop-out mechanisms and movement detectors that normally alert us to the fact

that something has changed. Without those we have to rely on memory across eye movements and—as these experiments show—memory for what we have just been looking at seems to be surprisingly poor.

But why are we surprised? The reason is probably this. We imagine that as we look around a scene we are taking in more and more of the picture with each glance until we have in our head a pretty good idea of what is there. This is how seeing feels, and this is how we imagine it must work. But if this is so, we ought surely to remember the railing and notice when the top disappears. The power of change blindness suggests that there must be something wrong with this natural theory of the way vision builds up, but it is not clear what.

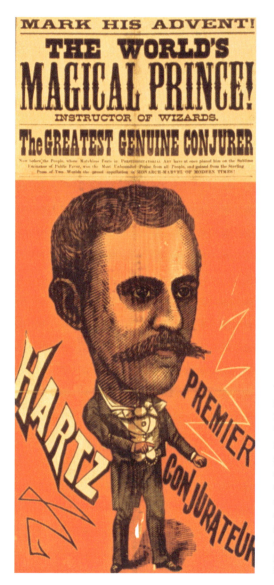

MARK HIS ADVENT!

THE WORLD'S
MAGICAL PRINCE!
INSTRUCTOR OF WIZARDS.

The GREATEST GENUINE CONJURER

Now before the People, whose Matchless Feats in Prestidigitation Art have at once placed him on the Sublime Eminence of Public Favor, won the Most Unbounded Praise from all People, and gained from the Sterling Press of Two Worlds the proud appellation of MONARCH-MARVEL OF MODERN TIMES!

HARTZ

PREMIER CONJURATEUR

Though magicians such as Augustus F. Hartz (1843–1929), "The Greatest Genuine Conjurer," have been playing tricks with attention for thousands of years, recent experiments with vision and attention indicate that we may be tricked all the time. This detail of a poster for the magician is from 1888.

INATTENTIONAL BLINDNESS

The strange phenomenon of inattentional blindness suggests that we may not see something at all unless we are paying attention to it. Psychologists Arien Mack and Irvin Rock held subjects' attention by asking them to watch a fixation spot and, when a cross briefly appeared, to decide whether one arm was longer than the other. When a highly visible object unexpectedly flashed close to the cross, most subjects failed to see it. Even more surprising was that when they had to attend to a cross slightly to one side of where they were looking, they failed to see the object flashed right in front of their eyes. It seems that paying attention to one side makes you blind where you are looking. Mack and Rock conclude that there can be no conscious perception without attention.

Magicians have played tricks with attention for thousands of years, but experiments like these suggest we may be tricked all the time. If this is true, it is very strange. It implies that when we look around the room we only see the very few things we pay attention to and—in spite of the way it feels—we do not really see anything else.

• • • • •

One possibility is that attention provides the key. So does paying careful attention to something save you from missing the change? Psychologists Daniel Levin and Daniel Simons put this to the test. They created short movies in which various objects disappeared or changed identity or color. In one movie the sole actor is sitting in a room and gets up to go to the door when the phone rings. There is a cut to outside the room and there a completely different person picks up the phone. Only a third of the observers detected the change.

You might think that this worked by some trickery in the film but, amazingly, Levin and Simons have demonstrated the same effect with ordinary people in everyday surroundings. In one case they arranged for an experimenter to approach a pedestrian on the campus of Cornell University and ask for directions. While the experimenter kept the pedestrian talking, two assistants dressed as workmen rudely barged in between them carrying a door. At that moment, the experimenter grabbed the back of the door and swapped places with the person who had been carrying it. The poor pedestrian was now confronted with a completely different person talking to him. Yet only half of the pedestrians noticed the substitution. Again, when people are asked whether they think they would detect such a change they are convinced that they would—but they are wrong.

There are implications here for ordinary life. For example, change blindness can be induced by using "mud splashes" or meaningless blobs that appear at the time of the change. This happens frequently on the road and in the air, suggesting that dangerous mistakes might be made by drivers or pilots if a crucial event occurs just as some mud hits the windshield, and this may well be the cause of some apparently inexplicable accidents. But here we are concerned with the implications for consciousness.

Grand Illusion Theory

The findings of change and inattentional blindness challenge the way most of us naturally seem to think about our own visual experiences: that is, if we believe that we have a rich and detailed stream of pictures passing through our consciousness one after the other, we must be wrong. This is the basis of what has come to be known as "grand illusion" theory—or the theory that the visual world is all a grand illusion.

How could we be so wrong? If we are, we need to understand how the illusion is perpetrated and why we fall for it. There are several different theories that try to explain the findings, all starting from the discovery that every time we move our eyes we throw away most of the available information. Obviously we have to keep some information; otherwise, the world would appear completely incomprehensible, so the theories differ in explaining how much and what sort of information we do retain when we look around the world.

According to Levin and Simons, we really do have a rich visual experience each time our eyes fixate on something, and from that we extract the meaning or gist of the scene. Then, when we move our eyes, the detail is thrown away and only the gist is retained. In this way we keep a firm idea of what we are looking at and can always see some part of it in detail. This, they argue, gives us a phenomenal experience of continuity without too much confusion.

Canadian psychologist Ronald Rensink has also done extensive research on inattentional and change blindness and has a somewhat different interpretation. He argues that the visual system never builds complete and detailed representations of the world at all, not even during fixations. Instead, it builds up representations of single objects, one at a time, as our attention shifts around. Whenever we attend to something, its representation is created and maintained for some time, but when we stop attending it loses its coherence and falls back into a soup of separate features. He explains that the reason we get the impression of a rich visual world is because a new representation can always be made just in time by looking again.

This seems very odd. It is hard to believe that when I am looking at my cat the rest of the room disappears from my visual system. But this is what Rensink's theory implies. And, after all, how could I check? If I try to look really quickly at something to, as it were, catch it out not existing, I am bound to fail, for as fast as I can look at it I am building up a new representation. My impression that I can see the whole room is correct, but this is because I can always look again, not because I have a picture of the whole room in my consciousness.

This is reminiscent of the trouble William James described more than a century ago in his explorations of consciousness. He likened introspection to "trying to turn up the gas to see how the darkness looks." I imagine he would enjoy doing the same with electricity, or with the modern equivalent of trying to open the fridge door really quickly to see whether the light is always on.

In the case of the fridge, we can easily check by leaving a camera inside, or making a hole in the side to look through. The equivalent with the brain is much harder, but neuroscience is making great progress in developing techniques of brain scanning. If we discovered that the visual system really does work this way, holding only a minimal amount of bound object information at a time, then we would have to conclude that there is nothing inside the brain that corresponds to the detailed stream of vision we think we are experiencing.

This has implications for the search for the neural correlates of consciousness. For example, Crick says that he wants to find the correlates of "the vivid picture of the world we see in front of our eyes," or what Damasio calls the "movie-in-the-brain." But if the visual world is a grand illusion, then they will never be able to find what they are looking for because neither the movie-in-the-brain nor the vivid picture exists in the brain. They are both part of the illusion.

There is one final theory that goes even further in demolishing our ordinary ideas about visual awareness. This is the "sensorimotor theory of vision" proposed by psychologist Kevin O'Regan and philosopher Alva Noë. They take a fundamentally new approach in which vision is not about building internal representations at all, but is a way of acting in the world. Vision is about mastering the sensorimotor contingencies— that is, knowing how your own actions affect the information you get back from the world, and interacting with the visual input to exploit the way it changes with eye movements, body movements, blinks, and other actions. In other words, seeing is action. In this view, vision is not about building representations of the world; instead, seeing, attending, and acting all become the same thing. In this view, what you see is those aspects of the scene that you are currently "visually manipulating." If you don't manipulate the world, you see nothing. When you stop manipulating some aspect of the world, it drops back into nothingness.

This kind of theory is dramatically different from traditional theories of perception, but is similar to theories of embodied or enactive cognition that are being developed in the field of artificial intelligence. In this case, people building robots have found that giving robots detailed and complex internal representations is an inefficient and even impossible way of getting them to move around in the real world. Instead, it is better to build in simpler systems that let them play with the world, make mistakes, and learn for themselves how to interact with it.

Does this approach help with understanding visual consciousness? Traditional theories, with their inner representations, could not

One recent theory states that vision is a way of acting in the world, so that what you see is what you are currently "visually manipulating," which is very different from traditional theories of perception but similar to theories that are being developed in the field of artificial intelligence. One facet of RoboCup, an international research and education initiative fostering artificial intelligence and robotics research, is a series of robot soccer matches. This 2007 photograph shows a match in the Four-Legged League, in which fully autonomous (guided by neither humans nor outside computers) robots compete. Are they conscious?

explain how those representations became conscious experiences, why some visual representations were "in" consciousness while most were not, or why we seem to be someone looking at the representations. Sensorimotor theory turns the problem upside down, making the viewer into an actor and the visions into actions. So now it must explain how actions can become subjective experiences. Whether this will prove possible we have yet to see, but it certainly changes the problem completely. Since the traditional theories lead only to confusion and the hard problem, it is worth taking seriously the idea that vision is a grand illusion.

Answer to riddle: Children brought them there to make a snowman, which melted in the sun. You may have had your own "eureka moment" when I mentioned a snowman on page 63, or the answer may just have popped up spontaneously—or not at all.

FIVE

The Self

•

Spirits and Souls

Who—or what—am I? Answers such as "I am my body" or "I am my brain" are unsatisfactory because I don't feel like a body or a brain. I feel like someone who owns this body and brain. But who could it be who feels as though she lives inside this head and looks out through the eyes? Who is it who seems to be living this life and having these experiences?

From the scientific point of view there is no need for an owner; no need for an inner experiencer to observe what the brain is doing; no need

The idea of the self comes from the feeling that there is someone who lives your life, looks out through your eyes, and has your experiences. Although this feeling is constructed by the brain, the self is often conceived of as separate from the body and the brain—and most major religions are proponents of some version of this theory. *The Spirit's Flight*, a hand-colored Currier & Ives lithograph from 1893, depicts a Christian illustration of the concept, with an angel hovering above two spirits in flight.

for an inner self. Brains may be complex and hard to understand, but they are "causally closed." That is, we can see how one neuron affects another, how groups of neurons form and dissipate, and how one state leads to another, and there is no need for any further intervention. In other words, my brain doesn't need "me."

Even so, I have this overwhelming sense that I exist. When I think about conscious experiences, it seems to me that there is someone having them. When I think about the actions of this body, it seems that there is someone acting. When I think about the difficult decisions of my life, it seems as though someone had to make them. And when I ask what really matters in this world, it seems as though things must matter to someone. This someone is "me," my true "self."

The question of self is intimately bound up with the problem of consciousness because whenever there are conscious experiences it is easy to assume they must be happening to someone, that there cannot be experiences without an experiencer. So we reach an impasse. Science does not need an inner self, but most people are quite sure that they are one. And in addition, many people believe that doing away with the idea of the self would unleash chaos, undermine motivation, and destroy the moral order. Much hangs on whether we believe in the existence of selves or not, yet our ideas about self tend to be deeply confused.

Philosopher Derek Parfit tries to sort out some of the confusion by distinguishing between ego theorists and bundle theorists. He starts from the undoubted fact that we *seem* to be single, continuous selves who have experiences, and asks why. Ego theorists reply that this is because it is literally true; we really are continuing selves. Bundle theorists, by contrast, reply that it is not true and the experience of self must be explained some other way.

Bundle theories take their name from the work of the philosopher David Hume (1711–76), who described how he stared into his own experiences looking for the experiencing self but all he ever found was the experiences. He concluded that the self is not an entity but is more like a "bundle of sensations"; one's life is a series of impressions that seem to belong to one person but are really just tied together by memory and other such relationships.

Note that dualism is only one form of ego theory, and you need not be a dualist to believe in a continuous self. Indeed, as we shall see, many

Eighteenth-century Scottish philosopher David Hume was the first to describe the bundle theory, that "I" am just a bundle of thoughts and sensations. Hume is shown here in an undated engraving from an original by G. Phillips.

modern scientific theories that reject dualism still attempt to find the neural correlates of the self or to explain the self in terms of enduring structures in the brain. So these are ego theories.

The major religions provide clear examples of each type. Almost all are straightforward ego theories, based on the assumption that selves exist, whether those selves are conceived of as souls, spirits, the atman, or anything else. The existence of such personal selves underlies doctrines about identity, life after death, and moral responsibility, and is central to the beliefs of Christians, Jews, Muslims, and Hindus. Although there are some scientists who are religious, and some who claim that there is no incompatibility between science and religion, the question of self is an obvious sticking point. If each person has a spirit or soul, as well as a brain, then science ought to be able to detect it, but so far it has not. This is not to say that it never will, but certainly there is a problem.

Among religions, Buddhism alone rejects the idea of self. The historical Buddha lived in northern India about twenty-five hundred years ago and supposedly became enlightened after long meditation under a tree. He rejected the prevailing religious doctrines of his time, including the eternal inner self or atman. Instead, he taught that human suffering is caused by ignorance and in particular by clinging to a false notion of self; the way out of suffering is to drop all the desires and attachments that keep re-creating the self. Central to his teaching, therefore, is the idea of no-self. This is not to say that the self does not exist, but that it is illusory—or not what it seems. Rather than being a persisting entity that lives a person's life, the self is just a conventional name given to a set of elements. He also taught that everything is dependent upon prior causes and nothing arises independently, as in the modern idea that the universe is interdependent

The Buddha denied the existence of persisting selves. This statue of the Buddha is located in the sixteenth-century Laotian temple of Haw Phra Kaew, in Vientiane.

and causally closed. This explains how he could claim that "actions exist, and also their consequences, but the person that acts does not." Parfit refers to the Buddha as the first bundle theorist.

Bundle theory is extraordinarily difficult to understand or to accept. It means completely throwing out any idea that you are an entity who has consciousness and free will, or who lives the life of this particular body. Instead, you have to accept that the word *self*, as useful as it is, refers to nothing that is real or persisting; it is just an idea or a word. And as for the self who has experiences, this sort of self is just a fleeting impression that arises along with each experience and fades away again. The illusion of continuity occurs because each temporary self comes along with memories that give an impression of continuity.

Such a counterintuitive theory would probably not be worth considering were it not for the enormous difficulty we must otherwise face in deciding just what a self is. The idea of self as an illusion is at least worth bearing in mind while we look at some of the stranger phenomena of selfhood.

Splitting Brains

What would it be like to have your brain cut in half? This may sound like a mere thought experiment, but in fact, in the 1950s and 1960s, this drastic operation was performed. Epilepsy can sometimes be so severe that life is made unbearable by almost continuous seizures. Today such cases can be treated with drugs or with less invasive surgery, but at that time the worst cases were treated by separating the two halves of the brain, so preventing the seizures from spreading from one side to the other. In most of these patients the main connection between the two hemispheres, the corpus callosum, was severed, leaving the brain stem and some other connections intact. So it is an exaggeration to say that their brains were cut in half, but without the corpus callosum most of the usual traffic between right and left hemisphere stops.

What happened? Remarkably, very little happened; the patients recovered well and seemed to live a normal life, with little or no change in personality, IQ, or verbal ability. But in the early 1960s, psychologists Roger Sperry (1913–94) and Michael Gazzaniga performed experiments that revealed some extraordinary effects.

The experimental design depends on knowing how the sense organs are connected to the brain. Information from the right ear goes

Neuroscientists Roger Sperry, who won the Nobel Prize in Medicine in 1981 for his work on the functional specialization of the cerebral hemispheres, and Michael Gazzaniga, a professor of psychology and the director for the SAGE Center for the Study of Mind at the University of California Santa Barbara, conducted experiments that revealed the effects of "splitting" the brain. Sperry is shown at left upon his receipt of the Nobel Prize, in Stockholm, and Gazzaniga is shown at right in a photograph taken in 2005 at Dartmouth College, in Hanover, New Hampshire.

to the right hemisphere (and left to left), but in vision, information from the left side of the visual field goes to the right hemisphere (and vice versa), as shown below. This means that if you look straight ahead, everything seen to the left goes to the right hemisphere and everything on the right goes to the left hemisphere. Things are also

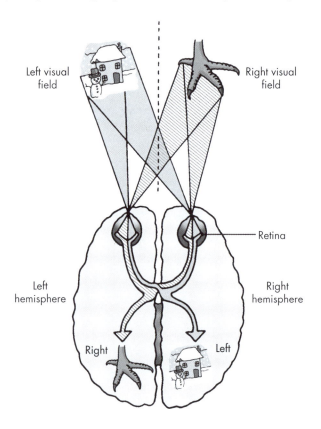

Cross-wiring of the human brain. Split-brain patient P. S. was shown a snow scene to the left and a chicken claw to the right. So the speaking left hemisphere could see only the chicken claw.

crossed over for the body, with the left half of the body controlled by the right hemisphere (and vice versa). In a normal person the two hemispheres are connected, so that information quickly gets through to both halves, but in a split-brain patient they are not. Knowing this, the experimenters could communicate separately with each of the two hemispheres of the one person. Would the two halves behave like two separate people? Was each independently conscious?

In a typical experiment the patient sat in front of a screen that was divided into two, and looked steadily at the center. Words or pictures were then flashed to one side or the other, thus sending information to only one hemisphere. The patient could respond verbally, or by using either hand.

Suppose that a picture was flashed to the right visual field. Since speech in most people is restricted to the left hemisphere, the patient could then describe it, quite normally, but if it was flashed on the left side, he could not. This showed that the left hemisphere, with its ability to speak, could only see what was shown on the right. Meanwhile, the right hemisphere could see what was on the left. This was revealed by asking patients to respond without words. For example, they could be given a pile of objects hidden in a bag and asked to select which had been seen using the left hand. In this way, the two hemispheres could simultaneously give different answers to the question "What can you see?" And neither seemed to know what the other was doing. Does this make them two conscious people?

In a famous experiment, the split-brain patient P. S. was shown a snow scene to the left and a chicken claw to the right and asked to pick out matching pictures from an array in front of him. With his left hand he chose a shovel (for the snow), and with his right hand a chicken. This makes sense in terms of what each half saw, but when asked to explain his reasons, he (i.e., the speaking left brain) said "Oh, that's simple. The chicken claw goes with the chicken, and you need a shovel to clean out the chicken shed."

In this way, the verbal left brain covered up its ignorance by confabulating. It did the same when the other half was shown an emotional picture—making up a plausible excuse for laughing, smiling, blushing, or whatever emotional reaction had been provoked. This might help to explain how these patients can appear so normal. But it should also make us wonder about ourselves. Our brains consist of lots of relatively independent modules, and the verbal part does not have access to everything that goes on, yet it frequently supplies convincing reasons for our actions. How many of these are plausible confabulations rather than true reasons, and can we tell?

From these experiments, Sperry concluded that his patients had two conscious entities in one head, each having private sensations and free will. In contrast, Gazzaniga argued that only the left hemisphere sustains "the interpreter," which uses language, organizes beliefs, and ascribes actions and intentions to people. Only this hemisphere has "high-level consciousness," leaving the other hemisphere with many abilities and skills but without true consciousness.

Which is correct? The trouble is that we have no idea how to find out. We can ask each hemisphere, but—as with other people, babies, or animals—we still cannot know for sure whether they are having conscious experiences as well as speaking and choosing pictures. This brings us right back to the arguments in Chapter 1. If you think that consciousness is an added extra, then you naturally want to know whether both halves have it or only one—but you cannot find out. Similarly, when it

WOULD YOU PRESS THE BUTTON?

Do you believe in the existence of selves? Does your heart tell you one thing and your intellect another? This philosophers' thought experiment is a good way to find out.

Imagine a machine that you can step inside and travel anywhere you wish to go. When you press the button, every cell of your body is scanned, destroyed, and re-created at your chosen destination. Since this is a thought experiment we must assume that the procedure is 100 percent safe and reversible. So you can have no legitimate fears about getting lost on the way. The question is—would you go?

If you are really a bundle theorist you should have no qualms at all. Every cell of your body will be just the same after the journey and all your memories will be intact. You will appear unchanged to everyone else, and you will have just the same illusion of an inner self as you had before.

If you still don't want to press the button, you must be clinging onto the idea that it won't really be "you" who arrives. In other words, you still believe in an inner self.

. . . . .

comes to selfhood—if you believe in the existence of persisting selves, then you naturally want to know whether both halves have a self—but you cannot find out.

This seems to matter. It seems to matter whether there is a second conscious self trapped inside the split-brain person and unable to speak properly or influence what is going on—it sounds terrible. But according to Parfit this whole problem is a fantasy provoked by believing in egos. Bundle theory does away with the problem altogether. There is neither one self nor two selves inside the split brain; there are experiences but there is no one who is having them—just as it is with you or me.

Hypnosis and Dissociation

Imagine the scene. You are at a show, and on the stage a man calls for volunteers to come and be hypnotized. Not daring to go yourself, you watch as lots of people raise their hands and the hypnotist slowly weeds them out with various games and tests until he has half a dozen or so ready for a "deep trance." Some minutes later, after suggestions of sleep, visualizing beautiful scenes, or imagining going down in an elevator, the volunteers are all slumped and ready for the fun. In no time, one is looking through imaginary clothes-removing glasses, another is behaving like a circus horse, and a third is roaming through the audience asking them to wake him up.

Or consider hypnosis as therapy. It is used to help people give up smoking, lose weight, reduce stress, or deal with emotional difficulties, and although many of the claims are exaggerated, some of these treatments help. Hypnosis is also used to reduce pain, and as an alternative to anesthetic in some kinds of operation.

Hypnosis emerged from the discredited Mesmerism, with its use of magnets and theories of "animal magnetism," and had its heyday in the late nineteenth century, when it was used in medicine and psychiatry, and for entertainment. Spiritualism was also popular at the time, and psychical researchers sometimes hypnotized mediums in order to

A phenomenon that seems to suggest a dissociation of the mind is hypnosis. Stage hypnotists have long provided entertainment by choosing members of the audience, hypnotizing them, and having them behave in silly ways. This undated poster advertising "MacKnight, Hypnotic Fun Maker" shows a man with a feather duster as a headdress doing a war dance, another playing an umbrella as if it were a violin, another trying to saw a chair with a cane, and two more behaving as if they were a coachman and horse.

dissociate their spirit from their body—just one of many phenomena that seemed to suggest a dissociation of the mind.

Another was the odd phenomenon of multiple personality. In 1898 a young woman, Miss Christine Beauchamp, suffering from pain, anxiety, and fatigue, consulted Dr. Morton Prince (1854–1929) of Boston. Prince hypnotized Miss Beauchamp, whereupon she changed into a very passive personality. Then a completely new personality appeared, and began referring to Miss Beauchamp as "she." Sally, as she came to be called, was lively, fun, outspoken, strong, and healthy; Christine was dull, nervous, weak, and exceedingly virtuous. When Christine wrote sensible letters, Sally would emerge only to tear them up. When Christine refused to smoke, Sally would take over and light up. In other words, Sally made life hell for Christine and yet they were both inhabiting the same body.

The case of Miss Beauchamp was one of the classics of multiple personality, and hundreds of cases were reported between 1840 and 1910. Psychiatrists, doctors, and researchers all believed that two or more distinct personalities could take over one body. William James, for example, thought that such cases, along with other hypnotic phenomena, proved that one brain could sustain many conscious selves, either alternately or at the same time. These were called co-consciousnesses or underselves.

The cases began to get more bizarre, with increasing numbers of personalities and no theory to explain what was going on. So in the early twentieth century there was a reaction against the idea, with experts claiming that the whole phenomenon had been created by hypnosis and by the persuasive power of male doctors over their obliging female patients. It was true that many were induced by hypnosis—and some were apparently cured again by hypnosis. However, some occurred spontaneously, and continued to fascinate people, as with the 1950s film *The Three Faces of Eve* and the popular 1970s story of Sybil, "a woman possessed by sixteen separate personalities."

These cases heralded a new epidemic, and by 1990 more than twenty thousand cases had been diagnosed in the United States, with television shows and books contributing to the spread of the idea. Once again, the profession became critical and the cases slowed down. In 1994 the term *multiple personality* was dropped in favor of the term *dissociative identity disorder*, and few professionals now refer to multiple personality at all.

What makes these cases seem so strange is the idea that the mind can be split or dissociated into separate parts. This same strangeness occurs with some other phenomena of hypnosis and has led to heated and still

Joanne Woodward plays a woman with multiple personalities—Eve Black, Eve White, and Jane—in *The Three Faces of Eve* (1957).

unresolved disputes. The traditional Victorian view was that hypnosis is a dissociated state in which part of the mind is cut off from the rest. The hypnotist takes over control by speaking directly to the dissociated part of the mind and causes the somnambulist (as they were often called) to behave and think differently, and even to perform feats that would be impossible in the normal waking state.

Since the nineteenth century, critics had objected that hypnotic trances were faked, or that hypnotic subjects were just complying with the experimenter or playing a role. This same argument carried on through most of the next century, with the arguments circling around one main question: Is hypnosis a special state of consciousness—perhaps a dissociated state—or not? "State theorists" say that it is, while "non-state theorists" say it is not.

There have been many attempts to test the two theories. The critical experiments compare hypnotized subjects with control subjects who are asked to fake being hypnotized, or to imagine and experience the hypnotic suggestions without any induction procedure. The argument is that if controls show the same phenomena as "really hypnotized" subjects, the idea of a special hypnotic state is redundant.

Many experiments have shown no differences between the groups, which tends to support non-state theory, and many psychologists are happy to conclude that there is nothing special about hypnosis. Even so, some oddities remain. For example, some hypnotic subjects show "trance logic" in which they will accept illogical or impossible situations in a way that controls cannot, such as seeing two versions of the same person at once, or seeing through objects to things behind them.

Another strange effect was found in the 1970s by psychologist Ernest Hilgard (1904–2001). Experiments had shown that good hypnotic subjects deny feeling pain when their hand is immersed in freezing water (a harmless method of inducing pain commonly used in psychology experiments). Hilgard believed that, deep down, some part of the person was still feeling the pain and so he said to his subjects, "When I place my hand on your shoulder, I shall be able to talk to a hidden part of you. . . ." When he did so the subjects described their pain and anguish. And in other experiments the "hidden observer" would describe apparently ignored stimuli, or forgotten events. It seemed as though someone else was having conscious experiences all along.

These findings led Hilgard to his neo-dissociation theory, arguing that in the normal state there are multiple control systems under the direction of an executive ego, but in hypnosis the hypnotist takes over, making actions feel involuntary and hallucinations real. This theory is not quite like the early dissociation theories in which separate parts of the mind were like separate conscious people, but it retains the idea that a single brain can sustain more than one set of conscious experiences at a time.

Needless to say, this theory is only one of many, and there is no unanimity. After more than a hundred years of research, we still do not know whether hypnosis involves a special state of consciousness or whether it can truly be said to divide consciousness.

Theories of Self

We can now return, a little more confused, to the question "Who or what am I?" All these phenomena challenge the usual assumption of one conscious self to one body, and leave us wondering how to explain both the exceptional cases and the normal sense of self. For if it is possible to have several conscious experiences going on at once, why do we feel ourselves to be unified?

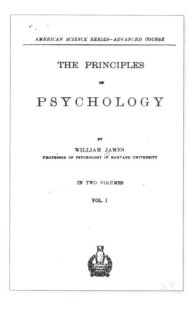

AMERICAN SCIENCE SERIES—ADVANCED COURSE

THE PRINCIPLES

OF

PSYCHOLOGY

BY

WILLIAM JAMES
PROFESSOR OF PSYCHOLOGY IN HARVARD UNIVERSITY

IN TWO VOLUMES

VOL. I

In his massive twelve-hundred-page, two-volume *Principles of Psychology* (1890), which took him twelve years to complete, American philosopher and psychologist William James agonized over the nature of the experiencing self.

There are numerous theories that attempt to explain the sense of self. There are philosophical theories on the nature of persons, personal identity, and moral responsibility; psychological theories of the construction of social selves, self-attribution, and various pathologies of selfhood; and neuroscientific theories of the brain basis of self. We cannot consider all of these here, so I have chosen a few examples that have obvious implications for consciousness.

William James's 1890 book *The Principles of Psychology* has been called the most famous book in the history of psychology. In two large volumes he tackles every aspect of mental functioning, perception, and memory, and agonizes over the nature of the experiencing self. He claims that this is "the most puzzling puzzle with which psychology has to deal."

James first distinguishes between the "me" which is the empirical self or objective person, and the "I" which is the subjective, knowing self or pure ego. It is the "I" that seems to receive the sensations and perceptions occurring in the stream of consciousness, and to be the source of attention and the origin of effort and will. But what could it be? James rejects what he calls the soul theory but also rejects the opposite extreme—the idea that the self is a fiction, nothing more than the imaginary being denoted by the pronoun "I."

His own solution is a subtle theory perhaps best understood with his famous saying that "thought is itself the thinker." He argues that our own thoughts have a sort of warmth and intimacy about them which he attempts to explain in this way: at any time there may be a special kind of Thought which rejects some of the contents of the stream of consciousness but appropriates others, pulling them together and calling them "mine." The next moment another such Thought comes along, taking over the previous ones and binding them to itself, creating a sense of unity. In this way, he says, the Thought seems to be a thinker. This sounds like an extraordinarily modern theory, entailing no persisting self or ego. However, James rejected extreme bundle theory and still believed in the power of will and a personal spiritual force.

One hundred years on, neuroscientists are taking up the problem. Ramachandran refers to his work on filling-in (Chapter 4), which seems to raise the question of who the picture is filled in for. Through this research he says, "we can begin to approach the greatest scientific and philosophical riddle of all—the nature of the self." Ramachandran suggests that filling-in is done not for someone but for something and that something is another brain process, a process in the brain's limbic system.

Global workspace theories take the same line of argument, equating self with particular groups of interacting neurons. For example, in Baars's theory, a hierarchy of contexts determines what gets into the spotlight in the theater of consciousness. Dominant among these is the self-system, which allows information to be reportable and usable. Multiple personality can be explained by different context hierarchies competing for access to the global workspace and to memory and the senses, but this does not allow for the kind of co-consciousnesses described by James and Hilgard.

Another example is Damasio's multilevel scheme. Simple organisms have a set of neural patterns that map the state of an organism moment by moment, and which he calls a proto-self. More complex organisms have core consciousness associated with a core self. This is not dependent upon memory, thought, or language and provides a sense of self in the here and now. It is a transient self, endlessly re-created for each object with which the brain interacts. Finally, with the capacity for thought and autobiographical memory comes extended consciousness and the autobiographical self. This is the self that is told in your life story; it is an owner of the movie-in-the-brain and it emerges within that movie.

All these theories have in common that they equate the self with a particular brain process. They may begin to explain the origin and structure of the self, but they leave the mystery of consciousness untouched. In each case, brain processes are said to be experienced by a self because they are displayed or made available to another brain process, but just how or why this turns them into conscious experiences remains unexplained.

Finally, a completely different approach is provided by Dennett. Having rejected the Cartesian theater, he also rejects its audience of one who watches the show. The self, he claims, is something that needs to be explained, but it does not exist in the way that a physical object (or even a brain process) exists. Like a center of gravity in physics, it is a useful abstraction. Indeed, he calls it a "center of narrative gravity." Our language spins the story of a self and so we come to believe that there is, in addition to our single body, a single inner self who has consciousness, holds opinions, and makes decisions. Really, there is no inner self but only multiple parallel processes that give rise to a benign user illusion—a useful fiction.

It seems we have some tough choices in thinking about our own precious self. We can hang on to the way it feels and assume that a persisting self or soul or spirit exists, even though it cannot be found and leads to deep philosophical troubles. We can equate it with some kind of brain process and shelve the problem of why this brain process should have conscious experiences at all, or we can reject any persisting entity that corresponds to our feeling of being a self.

I think that intellectually we have to take this last path. The trouble is that it is very hard to accept in one's own personal life. It means taking a radically different view of every experience. It means accepting that there is no one who is having these experiences. It means accepting that every time I seem to exist, this is just a temporary fiction and not the same "me" who seemed to exist a moment before, or last week, or last year. This is tough, but I think it gets easier with practice.

SIX

Conscious Will

•

Do We Have Free Will?

Hold out your hand in front of you and—whenever you feel like it, and of your own free will—flex your wrist.

Did you do it? If not you must have decided against bothering. Either way, you made a decision. You flipped your hand at a certain moment, or you did not do it at all. Now the question is, who or what made the decision or initiated the action? Was it your inner self? Was it the power of consciousness? This is the way it feels, but, as we have seen, there are serious problems with the idea of an inner self, and even if an inner self does exist, we have no idea how it could make the action happen.

Do we have free will? In this depiction of the parable "The Choice of Hercules," by French classical painter Nicolas Poussin (1594–1665), Hercules is visited by two nymphs—Pleasure, offering an easy life, and Virtue, offering a severe but glorious life—and he must choose between them.

So perhaps there were just a lot of brain processes, following one after another, that determined whether and when you flexed your wrist.

This certainly fits with the anatomical evidence. Much is known about the control of voluntary actions from experiments on both humans and other animals. When any voluntary act is carried out, such as flexing the wrist, many areas of the brain are involved. Roughly, the sequence is something like this: activity begins in the prefrontal region, which sends connections to the premotor cortex. This programs the actions, and sends connections to the primary motor cortex. The motor cortex then sends out the instructions that move the muscles.

Other areas are involved in specific actions. For example, in speech, Broca's area produces the motor output and, in most right-handed people, is in the left hemisphere. Then there is the supplementary motor area, which deals with the precise sequencing and programming of preplanned actions, and the anterior cingulated, which is involved in attending to emotions and pain as well as action. Finally, evidence from brain scans in humans shows that an area called the dorsolateral prefrontal cortex is uniquely associated with the subjective experience of deciding when and how to act.

So the problem is this. Science can reveal which neurons are active as sensory information comes in, and when actions are planned and carried out. Yet deciding to act doesn't feel like neurons firing, whether in the prefrontal cortex or anywhere else. It feels as though there is something else—my self, my consciousness—that makes me free to respond the way I want.

This is the classic problem of free will. David Hume called the problem of free will the most contentious of metaphysics. Indeed, it is said to be the most discussed problem in all of philosophy, going back to

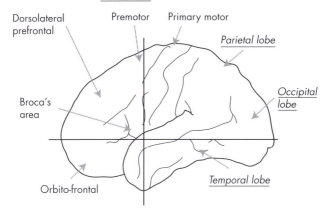

Lateral view of the left hemisphere
Frontal lobe

Dorsolateral prefrontal

Premotor

Primary motor

Parietal lobe

Occipital lobe

Broca's area

Temporal lobe

Orbito-frontal

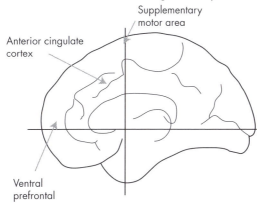

Medial view of the right hemisphere

Supplementary motor area

Anterior cingulate cortex

Ventral prefrontal

Brain areas involved in volition. When making a volitional act, neural activity flows from prefrontal areas through the premotor and motor cortex areas. Other areas marked here may also be involved. Where is the need for consciousness to intervene? How and where could an inner self act? (From S. A. Spence and C. D. Frith, Towards a functional anatomy of volition, *Journal of Consciousness Studies* 6, nos. 8–9 [1999]: 11–29. Reproduced by permission.)

the ancient Greeks and beyond. The issue raises strong feelings because freedom implies responsibility. We consider ourselves responsible, and we hold others accountable for their actions on the assumption that they freely chose to act the way they did. If there is no free will, then human moral responsibility might seem to be threatened, and with it the rule of law.

Part of the problem lies with determinism. To many early philosophers, as well as to modern scientists, the universe appears to be deterministic; that is, all events are determined by prior events. If this is so, the argument goes, then everything that happens must be inevitable, and if everything is inevitable there is no room for free will, because all my actions must be predetermined. This means that there is no point in my choosing to do anything, and no sense in which I could have done otherwise.

Some philosophers accept that free will and determinism are incompatible. They argue that either determinism is false (which seems unlikely and is extremely hard to prove) or free will must be an illusion (because it would amount to magic—an impossible nonphysical intervention). Note that the addition of truly random processes to a determined world, as in radioactive decay or quantum physics, does not provide a loophole for free will since these processes, if they are truly random, cannot be influenced at all.

By contrast, "compatibilists" find many varied ways in which free will and determinism can both be true. For example, some deterministic processes are chaotic. This means that they can have extraordinarily complex outcomes that cannot be predicted, even in principle, although they are entirely determined by the starting conditions. Also, humans have to make complex choices even in a determined world. Like other animals and some machines, human beings are complex agents and have to make lots of decisions. Indeed, they could not survive otherwise. For some compatibilists this kind of decision making is quite sufficient as a basis for moral responsibility and the law. And some are happy to count this as freedom of the will.

So where does consciousness fit in? In a way, it is consciousness that gives the whole problem its bite. For some people it is the human capacity for self-conscious thought that makes us different from other animals and machines; they believe that it is because we can consciously weigh up alternatives and consider the outcomes that we have free will and hence can be held responsible for our choices. Yet this brings us straight back to the same problem. If consciousness is conceived of as a force that makes free will possible, then it amounts to magic—an impossible intervention in an otherwise causally closed world. But if consciousness is not such a force, then our feelings of having conscious control must be an illusion. Some experiments may help us to decide which is right.

The Timing of Conscious Acts

Did you carry out that simple task of holding out your arm and flexing your wrist? If not, you should do so now—or do it again a few times—because this simple action is notorious in the psychology of voluntary action.

In 1985, Libet reported an experiment that is still argued about decades later. He asked the following question: When a person spontaneously and deliberately flexes his or her wrist, what starts the action off? Is it the conscious decision to act, or is it some unconscious brain process? To find out, he asked subjects to perform the wrist flexion at least forty times, at times of their own choosing, and measured the following three things: the time at which the action occurred, the beginning of brain activity in motor cortex, and the time at which they consciously decided to act.

The first two of these are easy to time. The action itself can be detected with electrodes on the wrist (electromyogram, or EMG). The start of brain activity can be measured using electrodes on the scalp (electroencephalogram, or EEG), which detect a gradually increasing signal called the "readiness potential," or RP. The difficulty comes in timing the moment at which subjects decided to act, which Libet called W for "will." The problem is that if you ask them to shout or press a button or do anything else, there will be another lag before this new action happens, just as there is with the wrist flexion. Also, the decision to shout may interfere with the main decision being measured. So Libet devised a special method for measuring W. In front of the subjects he placed a screen with a dot going round in a circle, like the hands of a clock. He then asked subjects to watch the clock and note where the spot was when they decided to act. They could then say, after the action was over, where the spot had been at that critical moment, and this allowed Libet to determine the time of their decision.

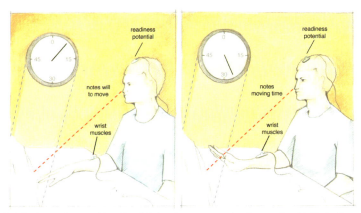

In Libet's experiment subjects flexed their wrist spontaneously, whenever they felt like it. He measured (1) the start of the readiness potential, (2) the start of the movement, and (3) the moment of willing, or the conscious decision to act. Which comes first?

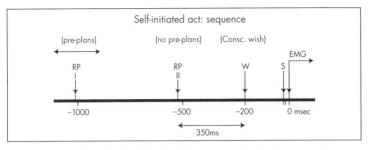

Libet's controversial results showed that the brain processes planning the movement began more than one-third of a second before the person had the conscious desire to move. (From B. Libet, Do we have free will? *Journal of Consciousness Studies* 6, nos. 8–9 (1999): 47–57, p. 51. Used by permission.)

So which came first? W or the start of the readiness potential? You might like to decide which answer you would expect, for this is likely to reveal your general views about self, consciousness, and free will.

Libet found that the decision to act, W, came about 200 milliseconds (one-fifth of a second) before the action, but the RP began about 350 milliseconds before that, or about 550 milliseconds before the action. In other words, the brain processes planning the movement began over one-third of a second before the person had the conscious desire to move. In brain terms this is a very long time. A lot of neural processing must have happened *before* the person consciously decided to move.

Perhaps it is not surprising that this finding has caused so much controversy. After all, it seems to threaten our most basic assumptions about willed action—that our decision to act starts the process off. And yet if you think about it, the idea of a conscious decision beginning before any brain processes would be nothing short of magic. It would mean that consciousness could come out of nowhere and influence physical events in the brain. The only theories that allow for this are dualist theories such as Descartes's, or Popper and Eccles's, and we have already seen why these appear hopeless.

This suggests that nobody should have been surprised by Libet's findings. Yet they were. Philosophers, neuroscientists, psychologists, and physiologists all entered into long and complicated disputes about what these results meant.

Some accepted the results at face value, concluding that consciousness comes too late to start the process of a voluntary action and therefore cannot be the ultimate cause. This, they concluded, shows that we do not have free will.

Among those who disputed this conclusion, some tried to reject the validity of the results, for example, arguing over the method for measuring W, the task used, or the experimental design, but Libet carried out many control experiments that ruled out most of the problems, and later replications have generally confirmed the findings.

Others argued that the results cannot be generalized to the kinds of action that matter for free will. For example, in this task the subjects could choose only *when* to act, not *which action* to perform. Also, a simple wrist movement is not comparable with a complex action such as getting out of bed or reading a book, let alone making a difficult choice such as whether to accept a job offer or how to bring up your children. In this way, people argued that Libet's results provide no evidence against the kind of free will that matters.

Libet himself did not accept these criticisms, nor did he accept that free will is an illusion. Instead, he found another role for consciousness in voluntary action. He had noticed that sometimes his subjects said they had aborted their movement just before it happened. So he carried out another experiment to test this and showed that in these cases the RP began as normal, but then flattened out and disappeared about 200 milliseconds before the action was due to happen. From this he argued for the existence of a "conscious veto." Consciousness could not initiate the wrist flexion, he said, but it could act to prevent it. In other words, although we do not have free will, we do have "free won't."

This, Libet argued, has important implications for freedom and responsibility. It means that, although we cannot consciously control our dispositions or impulses, we can consciously prevent them from being acted out. So, for example, we should not be held responsible for merely imagining wanting to kill, rape, or steal, because these impulses are not under conscious control—but we can be expected to prevent ourselves from doing such things because we have a conscious veto. In this way, Libet was able to accept his own findings without giving up on the power of consciousness. Indeed, he went further and developed the "conscious mental field theory," which posits that subjective experience is a unique and fundamental property in nature, a field that emerges from brain activity and can in turn act upon and influence that brain activity. He claims that this unified and powerful field explains the two most difficult features of consciousness—both the unity of our mental life and our sense of free will.

Finally, the sharpest criticism is that the experiment is entirely misconceived because it depends on the false idea that conscious experiences can be timed. As we saw in Chapter 3, experiments on time and consciousness have led to all sorts of muddles and conflicting conclusions. One way out is to take a thoroughly skeptical view about the idea of timing consciousness. Remember that Libet's experiment depends on timing the moment, W, at which the decision occurred in consciousness, or the moment at which it became conscious. But does it make sense to say that there is such a time?

The whole idea of timing conscious experiences is problematic because it assumes that there are two sets of timings: the times at which brain events happen, and the times at which those brain events "become conscious" or "get into consciousness." In other words, by accepting that the moment W can be timed, you are accepting that conscious experiences are something other than brain events.

An alternative is to reject the idea that conscious experiences are events that happen at particular times. This means interpreting the experiments rather differently. We might say that the subjects reported where the spot was when they knew that a movement was about to happen, but not that this was the time at which a decision was consciously made. In this view, conscious will cannot initiate actions, not because it comes too late, but because it is not something separate from the processes going on in the brain and so is not any kind of power or force at all.

The Feeling of Willing

All these arguments and experiments cast doubt on the idea that consciousness is the cause of our actions. Yet there remains the persistent feeling that it is. So it may be helpful to investigate just how this feeling comes about. When actions happen, we have to decide whether they are caused by ourselves or by someone else, and we can be wrong in two instructive ways.

First, we can do something and wrongly think someone else is responsible. In 1853, Michael Faraday (1791–1867), the physicist famous for his studies of electricity, carried out a decisive experiment on conscious control. At that time, in the mid-nineteenth century, the craze of spiritualism was at its height. From its beginnings in a small town in New York State, spiritualism had spread across Europe and America, and mediums

English chemist and physicist Michael Faraday is pictured here in an 1842 portrait by artist Thomas Phillips.

were putting on extravagant demonstrations of what they claimed were communications with spirits of the dead. One popular method of communication was called table tipping.

For this kind of séance, several sitters would gather round and place their hands flat on the table in front of them. The medium would then call upon the spirits to make themselves known, and the table would mysteriously begin to move. By asking the spirits to tap once for "yes" and twice for "no," or by using more elaborate alphabetical codes, questions were asked and answered, and the sitters went home believing that they had spoken with their lost parents, spouses, or children. In the most dramatic of séances, the table would not just tap with its legs on the floor but was reported to tip over, rise up on one leg, or even leave the floor altogether.

Naturally, accusations of fraud were rife, and some mediums were caught with hidden accomplices, telescopic sticks, or hidden strings. Yet some appeared to have no opportunity to cheat, or were even restrained by ropes and blindfolds during the performance. Faraday wanted to find out what was going on. After all, if a new force really was involved, the discovery could transform physics. If the consciousness of departed spirits could move a heavy table, then he wanted to know how.

To find out, he glued pieces of card onto the table with a soft cement that would give a little if the sitters' hands moved one way or the other. He reasoned that if the spirits were really moving the table, then the card would be found to have lagged behind the movement. But if the sitters were pushing and pulling, then the card ought to move ahead of the table. The results were clear. The card always moved farther in the direction the table moved. In other words, the sitters, not the spirits, were responsible.

Faraday questioned them closely and was convinced that they did not realize what they were doing. In further experiments he provided

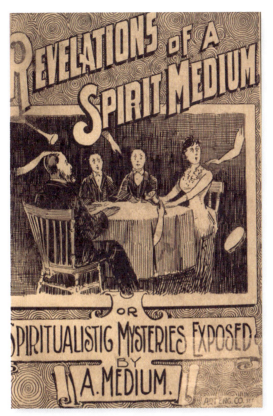

Faraday's experiments with séances showed that the sitters—not the spirits—were moving the table. The title page of *Revelations of a Spirit Medium*, published in 1891 in St. Paul, Minnesota, shows four spirit seekers at a séance table.

a gauge that showed how much sideways pressure they were putting on the card. When they could see the gauge, all the movements stopped. Faraday concluded, not that the sitters were cheating, but that they were using "unconscious muscular action"; the first demonstration that sometimes we can believe we are not doing something when we are.

The same principle applies to the more modern Ouija board, in which letters and numerals are placed around the edge of a table and the participants put their fingers on the bottom of an upturned glass. When asked questions, the glass seems to move without anyone consciously controlling it. This happens because the arm muscles tire quickly, making it hard to keep track of where one's finger is. When a slight movement occurs, each person adjusts his or her finger position, causing a much bigger movement. These sorts of adjustments are quite normal. Indeed, they are essential for keeping upright when we stand still, or holding a hot cup of tea safely in our hand. No muscles can keep absolutely still, so our body is in a perpetual state of slight movement with constant readjustment.

Note that the existence of unconscious muscular action does not imply that there is something called "the unconscious" which is the source of the movements. It need only imply that people can perform actions without realizing they are doing so because their body, with all of its multiple parallel control systems, just gets on with the job.

A much less amusing example of this sort of mistake occurs in schizophrenia. Schizophrenia is a serious psychiatric illness that occurs throughout the world and affects about 1 percent of the population. What makes it so devastating is the loss of the sense of personal control. The most common symptom of schizophrenia is auditory hallucinations, and many schizophrenics hear voices speaking to them. Some are convinced that spirits of the dead, elves living in the walls, or aliens from outer space are trying to communicate; some hear their own thoughts broadcast out loud for everyone to hear; some believe that other people around them are inserting thoughts into their minds. Experiments using brain scans have shown that the voices coincide with activity in the parts of the brain that would be activated if the person were imagining the voices, so we may safely assume that they are. Yet they are convinced that they are not. If it were possible to understand how this comes about, then effective treatment for schizophrenia would be much closer.

One final example of this mistake came about in a curious experiment carried out in the 1960s, when brain surgery often meant opening up the skull to provide access to large areas of the brain. The British neurosurgeon William Grey Walter (1910–77) had patients with electrodes implanted in their motor cortex as part of their treatment, and he

Neurophysiologist and robotician William Grey Walter created some of the first autonomous robots as part of his research into the workings of the human brain and behavior. In a time-lapse and multiple-exposure photograph taken in 1950, Walter is shown with two of his robots, Elmer (left) and Elsie (right), which have left light trails as they move autonomously around a chair and table.

investigated what happened when he asked them to control a slide projector. In some conditions, they could press a button, whenever they liked, to see the next slide. In others, Grey Walter took the output from their brain, amplified it, and used that signal to change the slide. The patients were quite perturbed. They said that just as they were about to press the button, the slide changed all by itself. Even though they were actually in control, they did not have the feeling of willing. Whatever else this tells us, it certainly shows that feelings of will can sometimes be wrong.

The Illusion of Conscious Will

Humans are extraordinarily quick to infer that the events they observe are caused by creatures with plans and intentions. Even very young children react differently to objects that move by themselves compared with those that are pushed or pulled by something else, and as they get older they develop what is called a "theory of mind," the understanding that other people have desires, beliefs, plans, and intentions. It is as though we are set up to detect living things and attribute actions to them. Indeed, this may be exactly what is going on, and the ability has probably evolved for good biological reasons. Survival could easily depend on correctly interpreting events as either irrelevant movements or the deliberate actions of another living creature.

Using this ability, people easily jump to the conclusion that events are caused by an agent when they are not. Indeed, the success of cartoons and computer games depends on this. It makes it possible to provide very crude representations of living things and still have your audience shouting for Jerry to escape from Tom, or poor Kenny not to be killed yet again. It also seems quite natural to talk about inanimate things as though they had minds. No one thinks it odd if I say "my watch thinks it's Thursday" or "this laptop is determined to ruin my lecture." Dennett calls this taking the "intentional stance." That is, we treat other people (or computers, clocks, and cartoon characters) as though they had minds, and this, he argues, is usually an effective shortcut for understanding what is going on.

We also turn the same habit on ourselves. Not only do we attribute desires and intentions to others, but we suppose that we have an inner self who has the same kinds of desires and intentions and who makes things happen. So when we get the feeling of having willed something, it is the feeling that "I" did it. As far as evolution is concerned, it does not matter that the center of will is a fiction, as long as it is a useful fiction.

As ever, we can learn a lot about the process from the occasions when it goes wrong. We have already considered examples in which people caused something but got no corresponding feeling of having done so. There are also occasions when the opposite occurs.

One example is called the "illusion of control" and is common in lotteries and games. If people are given a choice over the number of their ticket, they perceive their chances of winning as being higher, and if they do win they feel as though they contributed to the outcome. Similarly, casinos could probably not make any money were it not for the illusion of control, for it is the persistent feeling that one's actions make a difference that keeps people playing games of chance. Belief in the paranormal is also bolstered by the illusion of control. For example, if people try mentally to produce some outcome and it happens, they get a powerful sense of having caused it; if they think all evening of their friend and then she rings, they get a strong sense that their thoughts caused the call. These feelings can easily override any logical denial of the distant effects of thoughts.

· · · · ·

SUPERNATURAL BELIEFS

Why are humans so prone to believing in ghosts, spirits, and gods? Evolutionary psychologist Steven Pinker argues that in seeking to understand the weather, the heavens, or patterns of health and disease, we use brains and perceptual systems that evolved for other purposes. We simply cannot help adopting the intentional stance and so we imagine that someone must have caused the events we see.

The same natural tendency makes spiritualism and psychic demonstrations so beguiling. When psychologist Richard Wiseman reenacted Victorian séances, his sitters saw objects floating in the dark, felt touches on their skin, heard bells ringing, and were convinced that spirits had been moving among them. The phenomena were faked by a magician, yet even disbelievers fell for the tricks because when we see things moving we suspect someone must be moving them. When objects move just as they would if someone were walking around carrying them, then we imagine the person is there. In this way, ghosts and spirits are easily conjured.

· · · · ·

Even more powerful is the feeling that *our own* thoughts cause our actions. Psychologist Daniel Wegner likens experiences of conscious will to other judgments of causality. He proposes that free will is an illusion caused by making a big mistake. This illusion happens in three stages (though they may all occur very fast). First, our brain begins its planning for an action. Second, this brain activity gives rise to thoughts about that action. Third, the action happens and—

Casinos rely on people's belief that even in games of chance their actions somehow affect the outcome. In this photograph taken in Reno, Nevada, on October 8, 1910, men play a high-stakes game of faro before a crowd of spectators.

hey presto—we jump to the conclusion that our conscious thoughts caused the action.

So let's suppose that you decide to pick up the phone and ring your friend. First, brain activity begins to plan the action (presumably in turn caused by previous brain activity and external events). This brain activity gives rise to thoughts about ringing. Finally, your hand reaches out and picks up the phone. You jump to the false conclusion that your conscious thoughts caused the action.

Could it really work this way? Wegner has devised several experiments to find out. He suggests that there are three prerequisites for the experience of willing to occur: the thought must come before the action; the thought must be consistent with the action; and it must not be accompanied by other causes. To test these proposals, Wegner carried out an experiment inspired by the traditional Ouija board which, like Faraday's tipping tables, depends on unconscious muscular action. In Wegner's version, the glass was replaced by a little board mounted on a computer mouse. Two players put their fingers on the board and it moved a cursor over a screen showing about fifty small objects. They heard words through headphones and had to keep the mouse moving until they heard a signal to stop. In fact one was a confederate and manipulated the stop, enabling Wegner to show that under certain conditions subjects were absolutely sure they had stopped the mouse themselves when in fact it had been done by someone else. This happened, as Wegner had predicted, when they had heard the name of the object just before the stop.

Wegner claims that the illusion of conscious will works just like a magic trick and arises for the same reason. Magicians can force their audience to believe they chose the card or thought up the number themselves, and we can all be tricked in ordinary life. He concludes that believing our conscious thoughts cause our actions is a delusion. Whether you agree or not, these demonstrations of the mistakes we make show one thing for sure—that the *feeling* of willing something is no evidence either for or against free will.

If you do agree, and you conclude that free will is an illusion, how can you or should you live your life? Some people conclude that there is no point in doing anything and they might as well give up. But this does not follow from the argument; nor is it easy to carry out. If you think you may as well give up, then ask yourself just what you will do, for you have to face the fact that you cannot simply do nothing. Staying in bed all day is not doing nothing, and you are bound to get up for food or the toilet. Ending your life is not doing nothing, and is neither easy nor enjoyable.

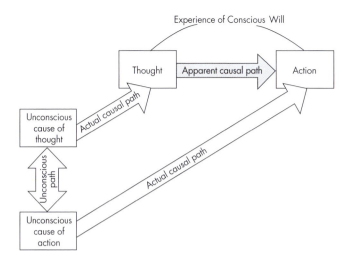

The illusion of conscious will. Wegner suggests that unconscious processes give rise to both thoughts about action and the action itself. We then wrongly infer that our thoughts cause our actions. (Wegner, Daniel M., *The Illusion of Conscious Will*: "Theory of conscious will," © 2002 Massachusetts Institute of Technology, by permission of The MIT Press.)

By facing up to how life might be without a belief in free will, it is easier to let go of the illusion.

Then what? Even if free will is, technically, an illusion, it is a very powerful illusion and so the feeling of being free carries on, even for people who no longer believe it is true. Such people sometimes say that they live "as if" free will existed, and "as if" they and others had selves. That way they can live honestly, without believing in something they know cannot possibly be true. For others, the feeling finally disappears.

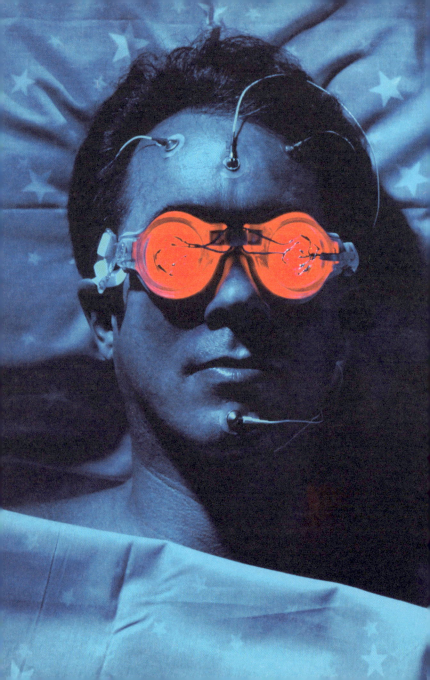

SEVEN

Altered States of Consciousness

•

Sleep and Dreams

Everyone dreams, though some people claim never to. The proof is easy to come by. If a self-professed nondreamer is woken up when his or her brain is showing the characteristic signs of REM (rapid eye movement) sleep, then that person will almost certainly report a dream. So the non-dreamer is really just forgetful; it is dream recall that varies widely, rather than dreaming itself. Another way to demonstrate this is to give the non-dreamer a pencil and paper and ask that person, every morning, to write down any recollections he or she has on waking. Anyone can do this, and the usual effect is a dramatic increase in dream recall. Within a few days

Everyone dreams, whether they remember their dreams or not. Dr. Steven LeBerge, professor at Stanford University in Palo Alto, California, and author of *Exploring the World of Lucid Dreaming*, uses goggles that signal that he is dreaming during REM sleep.

most people find themselves swamped by dreams and quite happy to go back to a little less reliable recall.

In a typical night's sleep the brain cycles through four stages of non-REM sleep, first going down through stages one through four, then back up to stage one, and then into a REM period, repeating this pattern four or five times a night. If people are woken at the different stages they describe different experiences. In REM sleep they will usually, though not always, say they are dreaming, while in non-REM sleep they may describe thinking, mulling something over, watching rather static images, or nothing at all. Children, and even babies, show the same physiological stages, but the capacity for complex and vivid dreams develops only gradually, as cognitive skills and imagination develop.

A great deal is known about the physiology of sleep and some of the ways in which it can go wrong. But this knowledge hides a much less certain picture when it comes to considering sleep as a state of consciousness.

Like much to do with consciousness, the notion of states of consciousness and altered states of consciousness (ASCs) seems superficially obvious. For example, we all know that it feels different from normal to be drunk or delirious with fever, and we may guess, even without experiencing it, that it feels different again to be high on drugs, or to be in a mystical state. So we can call all these ASCs.

Yet any attempt to define ASCs immediately runs into trouble. There are two obvious ways to try. First, there are objective measures, such as how much alcohol a person has drunk, or which method of hypnosis was used on them. This is not ideal because two people may drink the same amount and one become completely inebriated while the other is hardly affected. Similarly, induction techniques affect different people differently, and some not at all. Few states of consciousness are associated with unique physiological patterns, and measuring brain states gives confusing results. Measures of behavior can be unhelpful because people can claim to have been in profoundly altered states without their behavior apparently changing at all. In any case, all these objective measures really seem to miss the point that an altered state is how you feel it is, and is something private to the person having it.

For this reason, subjective definitions are usually preferred. For example, psychologist Charles Tart defines an ASC as "a qualitative alteration in the overall pattern of mental functioning, such that the experiencer feels his consciousness is radically different from the way it functions ordinarily." This certainly captures the idea of ASCs but also creates problems, such as knowing what a "normal" state is, and dealing with cases in which people are obviously (to anyone else) in a strange state but claim to feel completely normal.

Also, curiously, this definition hits a problem when we look at the most obvious state of all—dreaming. One of the most characteristic features of an ordinary dream is that we do not feel that our "consciousness is radically different"—at least not at the time. It is only afterwards that we wake up and say "I must have been dreaming." For this reason, some people even doubt that dreams can be counted as experiences. After all, we do not seem to be *experiencing* them at the time—only *remembering* them afterward. So did they really happen as they seemed to or might they have been concocted at the moment of waking up? And can we know?

Interestingly, there are ways of finding out. For example, it is possible to incorporate features into people's dreams by, for example, playing sounds to them or dripping water on their skin. Sometimes they will later report having dreamed of church bells or waterfalls. By asking them to estimate the timing of these events, it has been shown that dreams do take about the time they seem to.

An even better method is to use those rare people who can have lucid dreams at will. A lucid dream is when you know, during the dream, that it is a dream. In surveys, about 50 percent of people claim to have had a lucid dream, and 20 percent have them fairly frequently. For those who have never had one they sound rather strange. A typical lucid dream starts when something peculiar happens and the dreamer starts to have doubts—how did I get on top of this building, and why is my grandmother here when I thought she was dead? Instead of accepting the peculiarity, as we usually do in dreams, the dreamer realizes it cannot be real. With that realization everything changes. The dream scenery seems more vivid, the dreamer feels more like his or her normal waking self, and may even take control of the dream. At this point many people start to fly and have fun, but lucid dreams rarely last long and most people lapse back into the ignorance of ordinary dreaming very quickly.

A few, very rare, expert lucid dreamers have taken part in laboratory experiments and learned to signal from their dreams. In REM sleep almost all of the body's muscles are paralyzed—otherwise, you would act out your dreams—but the eyes still move and breathing carries on, so lucid dreamers can sometimes signal by moving their eyes. This allows experimenters to time their dreams and to observe brain activity during the dreams. Generally speaking, this confirms the realistic timing of dreams and also shows that the brain is behaving very much as it would if the person were really running down the street, playing tennis, singing a song—or whatever they are dreaming about. The difference is that they are not physically doing it.

This REM paralysis has another consequence. Sometimes people wake up before the paralysis has worn off and find they cannot move. This is known as sleep paralysis and can be a very frightening experience if you don't know what it is. Often it includes rumbling or grinding noises, eerie lights, and the powerful sense that there is someone close by. Most cultures have their sleep paralysis myths, such as the Old Hag of Newfoundland who comes and sits on people's chests in the night, or the incubus and succubus of medieval lore. Alien abduction experiences may be the modern equivalent—a vivid experience concocted in that unpleasant paralyzed state between waking and dreaming.

In sleep paralysis all the body muscles are paralyzed and only the eyes can move. One depiction of a sleep paralysis myth is shown here in Nicolai Abraham Abildgaard's 1800 painting *The Nightmare*, in which a demon or incubus appears in the night and crushes the sleeper's chest to prevent her from moving.

· · · · ·

ARE DREAMS EXPERIENCES?

There is no generally accepted theory of dreams, and some very odd facts to be explained. For example, on waking up, we remember having had dreams of which we were not conscious at the time. While experiments suggest that dreams go along in real time, many anecdotes describe dreams that were concocted at the moment of waking up. The most famous is that of the French physician Alfred Maury (1817–92), who dreamed of being dragged through the French Revolution to the guillotine only to wake up with the bed head falling on his neck.

One theory allows both these to be true. During REM sleep numerous brain processes go on in parallel, and none is either "in" or "out" of consciousness. On waking up, any number of stories can be concocted backward by selecting one of many possible threads through the multiple scraps of memory that remain. The chosen story is only one of many such stories that might have been selected. There is no actual dream, no story that really happened "in consciousness." In this "retro-selection" theory, dreams are not streams of experiences passing through the sleeping mind.

· · · · ·

Drugs and Consciousness

The effects of drugs on consciousness provide the most convincing evidence that awareness depends on the brain. This may seem obvious, but I mention it because there are many people who believe that their mind is independent of their brain, and can even survive after its death. This kind of theory becomes very awkward to sustain once you begin to understand the effects of psychoactive drugs.

Psychoactive drugs are those that affect mental functioning. They are found in every known culture, and human beings seem to take endless delight in finding ways to change their consciousness. Many psychoactive drugs can be dangerous, or even lethal, if wrongly used, and most cultures have a complex system of rituals, rules, and traditions that limit who can take which drugs, under what circumstances, and with what preparation. An exception is modern Western culture, where prohibition means that such natural protective systems cannot develop, and many of the most powerful psychoactive drugs are bought on the street and taken by young people without any such understanding or protection.

There are several major groups of psychoactive drugs and these have different effects. Anesthetics are those used to abolish consciousness altogether. The first anesthetics were simple gases, such as nitrous oxide or "laughing gas," which in high doses induce unconsciousness but in low doses are claimed by many to promote mystical states and philosophical insights. Modern anesthetics usually consist of three separate drugs to reduce pain, induce relaxation, and abolish memory, respectively.

One might think that studying anesthetics would be a good way to understand consciousness; we might find out what consciousness is by systematically increasing and decreasing it. In fact, it is clear that anesthetics work in many different ways, but mostly they affect the entire brain; there is no sign of a "consciousness center" or a particular process that is switched on and off.

Other psychoactive drugs are used in psychiatry, including antipsychotics, antidepressants, and tranquilizers. Some tranquilizers have become drugs of abuse, as have other depressants, that is, drugs that depress the central nervous system. These include alcohol (which has both stimulant and depressant effects) and barbiturates. Narcotics include heroin, morphine, codeine, and methadone. These mimic the action of the brain's own endorphins, chemicals involved in stress and reward. They are intensely pleasurable for some people but highly addictive.

Stimulants include nicotine, caffeine, cocaine, and amphetamine. Most of these are highly addictive; increasing doses are required to have the same effect, and withdrawal causes unpleasant symptoms and craving for the drug. Cocaine is normally inhaled into the nose but can also be converted to "crack" and smoked, which means it is faster acting and therefore more powerful and more addictive. The amphetamines are a large group including many of the modern designer drugs. An example is MDMA, or ecstasy, which has a combination of stimulating and hallucinogenic, as well as emotional, effects.

The most interesting drugs, from the point of view of understanding consciousness, are the hallucinogens. The term *hallucinogen* may not be entirely appropriate, because some of these drugs do not produce hallucinations at all. Indeed, technically, a true hallucination is one that the experiencer confuses with reality—as when a schizophrenic genuinely believes that the voices she hears in her head are coming from the walls of her room. In this definition, most hallucinogenic drugs produce "pseudohallucinations," because the user still knows that none of it is real. For this reason, these drugs are also known as psychedelic, which means mind manifesting, or psycholytic, which means loosening the mind.

Cannabis is in a class of its own, and is sometimes called a minor psychedelic. It is derived from the beautiful plant *Cannabis sativa*, or hemp, which has been used for over five thousand years both medicinally and as a source of tough fiber for ropes and clothes. Many nineteenth-century artists used cannabis for their work, and Victorians used it for medicine. It was made illegal in many countries in the twentieth century, but despite this is now widely used; it is usually smoked, either as grass (the dried leaves and female flowering heads) or as hash (a solid mixture of resin scraped from the plant, together with pollen, and powdered leaves or flowers). Hash can also be eaten raw, cooked, or dissolved in alcohol or milk.

The main active ingredient is delta-9-tetrahydrocannabinol, but cannabis contains over sixty other cannabinoids and many other constituents that have slightly different effects on the brain and the immune

The drug *Cannabis sativa,* or marijuana, is used recreationally by many people the world over. There are now known to be dozens of active ingredients which affect the brain in different ways to produce a variety of altered states of consciousness.

system, and may also interact with each other. Most are fat soluble and can remain in the body for days or even weeks. The effects of cannabis are hard to describe, partly because they are complex and variable, and partly because users say that words are inadequate to explain what happens. Some people become paranoid when smoking cannabis, and this seems to be increasing as stronger varieties of the plant are being bred. However, for most people the effects are fairly subtle and include relaxation, enhancement of the senses, increased pleasure in simple sensations, a tendency to laugh, increased sexual pleasure, openness to others, slowing of time, and various effects on memory. Experiments show that motivation is reduced and short-term memory is badly impaired, but the effects are usually temporary.

The 1936 film *Tell Your Children* was originally made as a cautionary tale, to be shown to parents in an effort to warn them about marijuana and keep their children away from it. It resurfaced in the 1970s as an unintentional comedy titled *Reefer Madness* and is now considered a cult film. Dorothy Short played teenager Mary Lane.

It is perhaps curious that the effects of this most widely used recreational drug sound so nebulous. We certainly have no science of consciousness that can adequately explain what happens to a person's consciousness when they smoke cannabis or why it is so pleasurable to so many.

The major hallucinogens have far more dramatic effects, are usually much longer lasting, and are harder to control, which perhaps explains why they are less widely used. They include DMT (dimethyltryptamine, an ingredient of the South American visionary potion, ayahuasca), psilocybin (found in "magic mushrooms"), mescaline (derived from the peyote cactus), and many synthetic drugs including LSD (lysergic acid diethylamide), and various phenethylamines and tryptamines. Most of these drugs resemble one of the four major brain neurotransmitters, acetylcholine, noradrenaline (norepinephrine), dopamine, and serotonin, and interact with their function. They can all be toxic at very high doses, and can exacerbate preexisting mental illness, but they are not generally addictive.

The best-known hallucinogen is probably LSD, which became famous in the 1960s when people were urged to "turn on, tune in, drop out." LSD induces a "trip" that lasts about eight to ten hours, so named because the hours seem endless, and often feel like a great journey through life. Not only are colors dramatically enhanced, but ordinary objects can take on fantastic forms: wallpaper becoming writhing colored snakes, or a passing car turning into a dragon with fifty-foot wings. Such visions can be delightful and glorious or absolutely terrifying—leading to a "bad trip." There is often a sense of the numinous, along with mystical visions, and a loss of the ordinary sense of self. A person can seem to become an animal or another individual, or to merge with the entire universe. An LSD trip is not a journey to be undertaken lightly.

In 1954, Aldous Huxley (1894–1963), author of *Brave New World*, took mescaline for the first time and described it as an opening of the "doors of perception." Ordinary things appeared colorful and fantastic; everything around him became miraculous and the world appeared perfect in its own "isness." His descriptions resemble those of mystical experiences, and indeed some people describe such drugs as "entheogens," or releasers of the God within.

This raises the interesting question of whether drugs can induce genuine religious experiences. In a famous study, American minister and physician Walter Pahnke gave pills to twenty divinity students during the traditional Good Friday service. Half took a placebo and experienced

English author Aldous Huxley became an advocate of psychedelic drugs. This photograph was taken in 1954, the year he first took mescaline. On his deathbed he asked his wife to give him LSD and he died peacefully.

only mild religious feelings, but half had psilocybin, and, of these, eight reported powerful mystical experiences. Critics dismiss these as somehow inferior to "real" mystical experiences, but this implies that we know what "real" mystical experiences are.

Unusual Experiences

From out-of-body experiences to fugues and visions, a surprisingly large number of people (perhaps 30–40 percent) report quite dramatic spontaneous altered states. These are sometimes known as "exceptional human experiences," especially if they involve a change in the person's sense of self or their relationship to the world.

Out-of-body experiences (OBEs) are those in which the person seems to have left his or her body and to be looking at the world from a location outside it. About 20–25 percent of the population claim to have had at least one such experience. It is usually very brief, although sometimes people report apparently flying great distances or going to other worlds. OBEs are usually pleasant, although they can be frightening, especially if they are combined with sleep paralysis.

Note that this definition does not necessarily imply that anything has left the body—only that the person feels as if it has. Theories differ widely on this point. For example, some people believe that their spirit, soul, or consciousness has left their body and may go on to survive the death of that body. According to the theory of "astral projection," a subtle "astral body" is exteriorized. Many experiments have been tried to test this idea but without success. For example, detectors have been used, including physical instruments, weighing machines, animals, and other people, but no reliable detector of an astral body or soul has ever been found. Alternatively, people having OBEs have been asked

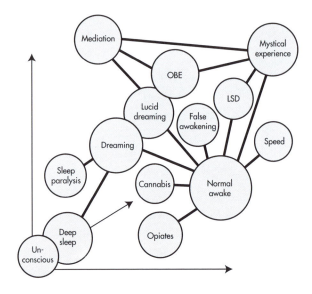

Can states of consciousness be mapped? Moving from one state to another can feel like moving in a vast multidimensional space, with some states easy to reach and others far away. Many people have tried to develop such maps, but it is hard to know what the relevant dimensions are.

to look at targets such as concealed numbers, letters, objects, or scenes. Although many claim to be able to see the targets, their descriptions are generally no more accurate than would be expected by chance. This does not prove that nothing leaves the body, but there is certainly no convincing evidence that it does.

Psychological theories explain OBEs in terms of how the person's body image and model of reality can change. It has been found that people who tend to dream in bird's-eye view or who are good at imagining changed points of view are more likely to have OBEs. OBEs can occur at almost any time, but are most common on the borders of sleep, during deep relaxation, and in moments of fear or stress. The experience has also been deliberately induced by electrically stimulating part of the brain's right temporal lobe, the region that constructs and controls our body image.

When people come close to death, they sometimes report a whole series of strange experiences, collectively known as a near-death experience (NDE). Although the order varies slightly, and few people experience them all, the most common features are: going down a dark tunnel or through a dark space toward a bright white or golden light; watching one's own body being resuscitated or operated on (an OBE); emotions of joy, acceptance, or deep contentment; flashbacks or a panoramic review of events in one's life; seeing another world with people who are already dead or a "being of light"; and finally deciding to return to life rather than enter that other world. After such experiences people are often changed, claiming to be less selfish or materialistic, and less afraid of death.

NDEs have been reported from many different cultures and ages, and seem to be remarkably similar in outline. The main cultural differences are in the details; for example, Christians tend to see Jesus or pearly gates, while Hindus meet ramdoots or see their name written in a great book. Religious believers often claim that the consistency of the experiences proves their own religion's version of life after death. However, the consistency is far better explained by the fact that people of all ages and cultures have similar brains, and those brains react in similar ways to stress, fear, lack of oxygen, or the many other triggers for NDEs.

All these triggers can cause the release of pleasure-inducing endorphins, and can set off random neural activity in many parts of the brain. The effects of this random activity depend on the location: activity in visual cortex produces tunnels, spirals, and lights (as do hallucinogenic drugs that have similar neural effects); activity in the temporal lobe induces body image changes and OBEs, and can release floods of memories; and activity in other places can give rise to visions of many kinds, depending on the person's expectation, prior state of mind, and cultural beliefs. There is no doubt that many people really are changed by having an NDE, usually for the better, but this may be because of the dramatic brain changes, and because they have had to confront the idea of their own death, rather than because their soul has briefly left their body.

One does not need to be near death to have profound experiences, and many quite ordinary people have quite extraordinary experiences in the midst of their everyday lives. These are usually called "religious experiences" if they include visions of angels, spiritual beings, or gods, but mystical experiences if they do not. There is no simple way to define or even describe a mystical experience. They are often said to be ineffable or indescribable, to involve a sense of the numinous, and to convey unexpected knowledge or understanding of the universe which cannot be spoken of. Perhaps most central to the experience is a changed sense of self, whether this is a complete loss of the idea of a separate self or a sense of merging with the universe in oneness.

These experiences usually occur spontaneously and are very brief, but there are methods that can make them more likely, or can gradually bring about similar states of mind.

Meditation

The common image of meditation is sitting cross-legged and going into a state of deep relaxation, cut off from the world. Some meditation is like this, but there are many different kinds, including walking meditations, and alert and active forms.

Meditation used to be practiced primarily within the context of religions, most notably in Hinduism and Buddhism, although the contemplative traditions in Christianity, Sufism, and other religions have similar methods. Today there are many secular forms of meditation, promoted mostly as methods of relaxation and stress reduction, the best known being Transcendental Meditation (TM).

Most meditation is done sitting down in special postures, such as the full or half lotus, in which both feet, or just one foot, rests on the opposite thigh. However, many people meditate in simpler positions, using firm cushions, or sitting on a low bench with their feet tucked underneath.

The aim of the special postures used in meditation is to provide a position that is both relaxed and alert. A firm base and a straight spine encourage good breathing and an alert mind.

There is nothing magical about these positions. They all have the same aim; that is, to provide a posture that is both relaxed and alert. In meditation there are always two dangers; either becoming drowsy and falling asleep, or becoming agitated by distracting thoughts or discomfort. The special postures provide a firm base, a straight spine, and good breathing, and so help avoid both.

Now, what about the mind? Here techniques differ widely, although it is sometimes said that they all have in common the aim of dropping thoughts and training attention—and neither is easy. If you have never tried it, you might like to do the following exercise—just look down and think of nothing for one minute.

What happens? The instruction cannot be obeyed. Thoughts come pouring up from inside, attention is distracted by things happening outside, and there is rarely a moment of silence in the mind. Perhaps this is not surprising. After all, our brains evolved to cope with the world and keep us safe, not to go silent on command. Nevertheless, with extensive training it is possible to calm the mind and let go of all distractions.

Most kinds of meditation entail learning to drop unwanted thoughts. The best advice is not to fight them, nor to engage with them in any way, but just to let them go. This can be used as the entire method, but it is not easy and so various other techniques have been developed. Concentrative meditation uses something else to attend to, giving the mind something to do. This might be a mantra (a word or phrase repeated silently), as is used in TM, or it might be an object such as a stone, flower, candle, or religious icon. The most common method is to watch the breath. The idea is simply to observe one's natural breathing, feeling the air going in and out, and then count the breaths up to ten. When you get to ten you go back to one and start again.

Other kinds of meditation use no support. For example, in Zen it is common to sit with eyes half open and look at a white wall. The aim in this case is "just sitting"—not something many people can do. Meditation can be done with eyes closed or open. The danger of closing the eyes is either going off into grand fantasies without realizing it, or falling asleep. The danger of open eyes is getting distracted, although it is easier to stay alert.

What is the point of all this? Many people take up meditation because they think it will be relaxing and help them cope with stress. In fact, thousands of experiments have been done on the effects of meditation and the results are rather surprising. When standard measures of relaxation are taken, such as heart rate, breathing, oxygen consumption, skin conductance, or brain activity, meditation is found to be no more relaxing than sitting quietly and reading or listening to music. Indeed, it can even be highly arousing, for example, when unwanted thoughts keep coming up and the person struggles to keep a control on his or her emotions. Certainly in the short term, it seems that meditation is far from a quick fix, and if you want to reduce stress it is probably better to get more exercise than to meditate.

In the long term, however, the effects are more profound. Long-term meditators, that is, those who have been practicing for many years or even decades, do enter states of very deep relaxation. Breathing rate can drop to three or four breaths a minute, and brain waves slow down from the usual beta (seen in waking activity) or alpha (seen in normal relaxation), to the much slower delta and theta waves. But people who practice for many years are not usually just seeking a method of relaxation. Their reasons for meditating are usually either religious or mystical. That is, they meditate to seek salvation, to help others, or to obtain insight.

This is certainly so in Buddhist meditation, and in particular in Zen, which is a form of Buddhism that has few religious trappings and a reputation for using tough methods to reveal direct insight into the nature of the mind. Some Zen students practice silent illumination, learning to calm the mind so as to look directly into the nature of consciousness. Others use special stories or questions called koans. These are not usually questions that can be answered intellectually, or even understood in any ordinary sense. Rather, they are questions that provoke the questioner into a great state of doubt and perplexity, from which new insights can arise. The ultimate koan is probably "Who am I?," a question that turns back on itself and causes the meditator to look deep into immediate experience. Not finding an obvious "me" is only the first step of what can be a long journey.

In Zen practice people report many enlightenment experiences in which something breaks through and the world is seen in a new way, but these may be only transitory experiences, much like spontaneous mystical experiences. The ultimate aim is said to be complete enlightenment in which the illusions of duality (illusions of a separate self and of someone who acts) are completely gone.

Such practices raise fascinating questions for the science of consciousness. Could we study how the brain changes in such cases and thereby understand what is going on? Are there really progressions through stages or do different people take different routes? Do people really become more compassionate and less selfish after meditation, as is claimed?

And, perhaps of most interest, are any of their insights genuine? In both mystical experiences and long-term meditation, people describe seeing through the illusion of separate selfhood, or seeing the world as it truly is. Could they be right? Are these the same illusions that the scientific study of consciousness is struggling with? All we can say for the moment is that the study of consciousness is nowhere near sufficiently well developed to answer such questions, but at least we can begin to ask them.

EIGHT

The Evolution of Consciousness

●

IT'S A LOVELY DAY AND YOU ARE GAZING at a great oak tree in the forest. You see the green leaves rippling in the breeze, the dappled shade dancing on the forest floor, and the birds flying from branch to branch. Looking closer, you see the intricate pattern of bark on the trunk and catch a glimpse of a beetle scurrying to hide. You smell the earth, littered with acorns, and feel the damp air around you. This is your conscious experience. This is the tree for you.

But what is it like for the beetle, for those birds, for the hidden sleeping bats above, or the snake hiding in the grass? We want to know, and it seems reasonable to ask, what the world is like from the animal's point of view. The trouble is we cannot know. As we found when asking

A person's experience of an oak tree is easy to imagine, but the experience of the bird that nests in it or of the beetle running along the bark, or even of the tree itself, is not.

"What is it like to be bat?," it is no good just imagining you are a bat or a worm. This is the question of animal consciousness. There are really two separate questions here: one concerns which living creatures are conscious and in what way; the other concerns when and how consciousness evolved.

It may help to think about a range of creatures and ask whether they are conscious. Let's begin with a stone lying under the tree. Most people would agree that there is nothing it is like to be the stone, or indeed the lumps of earth lying around, or the pieces of bark that have fallen off the tree. Yet panpsychists believe that everything in the universe is conscious; so for them, there are no unconscious creatures, and consciousness was there from the start.

What about the tree itself? Most people would say that trees and other plants are not conscious, yet a case could be made that the first stirrings of consciousness came with having senses and interacting with the world, and trees can sense the world. They respond to gravity, light, temperature, and moisture. Speeding up a film of the tree emerging from its acorn, we would see the tiny seedling twisting and groping upward, its fresh leaves seeking the light, and we would be much more inclined to grant it the possibility of consciousness. Similar arguments apply to lichens, algae, and perhaps bacteria.

What should we put next? If several people try to line up organisms from the least conscious to the most conscious they will not agree. Some will put babies near the bottom because they have not yet learned much, while others will put them near the top because of their potential. Some will put chimpanzees high up because they are so similar to us, while others will argue that crows, whales, and dolphins are more intelligent and that intelligence is what counts.

Another consideration is the different senses animals have. Snakes, for example, have an acute sense of smell and some have special sensors to detect infrared, and so catch their prey. Birds have little or no sense of smell, but they can see ultraviolet light that humans cannot. In fact, many birds have a four-color visual system which gives them a much richer ability to see color than we have with our human three-color system. What is it like to see a color that humans cannot see? We cannot even imagine this because we have to use our visual brain to imagine with and it lacks any representation of ultraviolet colors.

Insects, meanwhile, have compound eyes with thousands of separate lenses rather than a single eye like birds and mammals. They too can see in the ultraviolet. Lots of insects have an acute sense of smell, using scented trails to lead others to food or communicating with each other using pheromones, and detecting these chemicals through their antennae. What is their experience like? What is it like to smell a rotting mouse corpse using a sensitive antenna? For a fly that lays her eggs in such a corpse it presumably smells extremely attractive. From learning about

Knowledge about the senses of animals and insects, such as the four-color visual system of many birds or the compound eyes of this green shield bug, leads to the conclusion that every creature must be having a different kind of experience, inhabiting a different world, or *Umwelt*.

the senses of other animals we must conclude that, in that forest, every creature would be having a completely different experience. They would each be inhabiting an entirely different world, or *Umwelt*.

We may still be tempted to ask which animals are conscious at all. On the one hand, consciousness could be an all-or-nothing phenomenon, with some creatures having it and others not. Descartes believed that only humans had souls, and so other animals were "unfeeling automata." On the other hand, consciousness might be a continuous variable, with some having more than others. Any viable theory of consciousness ought to specify which creatures are conscious, in what way, and why.

How can we find out the answer? We hit again that curious feature of consciousness that we cannot know; there is no consciousness-detecting machine, no inner sanctum of consciousness production in the brain that we might find in some animals and not others. So the question remains unanswerable, and if a question is unanswerable it may be best to stop asking it.

Yet this one will not go away, if for no other reason than that we care about animal suffering. An unconscious automaton cannot suffer. So if Descartes and his successors are right, then we need not worry about animal pain. Yet animals appear to suffer. A cat with thick, shiny fur, bright eyes, and in a playful mood, seems obviously happy; a cat with thin, bedraggled fur, dull eyes, and limping from a bleeding gash on its leg, seems obviously to be in pain. Yet can we be sure our intuitions are correct?

Such intuitions are notoriously fickle. For example, people typically attribute more feelings to animals that are soft and cuddly and look like us, such as cats and rabbits with their forward-looking eyes. People will adopt the intentional stance toward anything that moves in a purposeful way, even the simplest robot; and experiments with more complex robots show how readily people will attribute emotions to a metal head that mimics smiling, frowning, or listening. We cannot trust these intuitions.

To break through this impasse, biologist Marian Stamp Dawkins argued that if an animal is really suffering it should be willing to work to avoid the cause of its distress. Concerned about battery hens provided with no litter to scratch in, she devised an experiment in which they had to push aside a heavy curtain to reach a cage with litter. Although they clearly preferred the cage with litter, they would not make an effort to get there. Behavioral measures like this can help us gauge the extent of animals' suffering, but may still leave some people saying "Yes, but is it just behaving as though it hurts or is it *really* feeling the pain?"

The best way to answer this would be to have a theory about just what abilities and behaviors imply consciousness and which do not, and in the case of animal consciousness there are several such theories.

Mirrors, Selves, and Other Minds

Look in a mirror and what do you see? Yourself of course. This may seem trivial, but in fact is quite an accomplishment. To be able to see yourself means that you must have a sense of self, and this is why mirror self-recognition has become such a well-known test. If being conscious relies on having a sense of self, as some people argue, then the mirror test might tell us something about animal consciousness. We need to find out which animals can recognize themselves in a mirror.

As any pet owner will attest, cats, dogs, and rabbits cannot. On first seeing a mirror, they may rush up to it with interest, and even look around the back for the other dog or rabbit they can see, but they soon get bored. Some fish will fight their own reflections, and birds will display to them. They obviously assume that they are seeing another fish or bird. But what about monkeys and apes?

In 1872, Charles Darwin (1809–82) tried giving a mirror to two young orangutans in the zoo, and described how they played and tried to kiss their reflections, but he could not be sure that they recognized themselves. Over a century later, psychologist Gordon Gallup devised a test to find out. He gave a group of young chimpanzees plenty of practice with mirrors; then he anesthetized them and painted two obvious red spots above one eye and the opposite ear. When they awoke, he let them look in the mirror. You or I, in such a situation, would immediately see the marks

Charles Darwin is shown in a photograph taken ca. 1870. When he placed a mirror on the floor between two young orangutans in the zoo, they tried to kiss the reflection as though it were another orangutan, experimented with various positions and grimaces, and then got angry and refused to look anymore. Darwin was the first to describe the similarities in emotional expression between humans and other animals.

Mirror self-recognition is used as a test for self-awareness. In Gallup's experiments chimpanzees tried to rub off a red spot that was placed so that they could see it only in the mirror.

and probably try to touch them or rub them off. So did the chimpanzees. They touched the spots more often than they touched the same place on the opposite side of their face.

Many other species have since been tested. Human children pass the test from about eighteen months onward. Of the four other species of great ape, chimpanzees, bonobos, and orangutans mostly do touch the spots, although they vary a lot, but gorillas do not. Tests with monkeys have shown no self-recognition, even though they can use mirrors in other ways, such as for reaching things they can see only in a reflection. This suggests a great divide between the great apes and the rest, but there are many doubts and problems. For example, some whales and dolphins are extremely intelligent, enjoy playing with mirrors, and may have a concept of self, but they have no hands with which to touch a spot.

This test, interesting as it is, provides no firm answers about consciousness. Gallup, who devised it, is convinced that chimpanzees not only recognize themselves in mirrors but have a concept of self, a notion of a personal past and future, and self-awareness. Skeptics agree only that chimpanzees can use their reflection to inspect their body and argue that this does not imply self-awareness.

Another way of getting at self-awareness is to investigate animals' social intelligence, including whether they can appreciate that others have minds. The idea here is that if an animal has a theory of mind, as humans do, then it can probably turn that understanding inward and see itself as having desires, intentions, and feelings. Deception is also relevant here because in order to deceive someone else you have to take account of what they know or want. Chimpanzees have been observed distracting others while they grab food, or hiding behind rocks to indulge in illicit behavior, but some clever experiments by primatologist Daniel Povinelli cast doubt on the extent of their social insight.

Chimpanzees naturally beg for food from humans and from each other. So Povinelli tested them under some rather odd conditions. In one experiment, two experimenters offered food to the chimpanzees, one with a blindfold over her eyes and one with another over her mouth. This made no difference to the chimpanzees; they begged equally to both. They even begged just as enthusiastically to an experimenter with a bucket over her head. It seems they have no idea that it is pointless to beg from someone who cannot see you. The conclusion for now is that chimpanzees do not have a theory of mind, but even this is still uncertain, and the implications for animal consciousness are more uncertain still.

One final dividing line is language, and here humans seem to be unique. It is important here to distinguish between true language and other forms of communication. For example, vervet monkeys make at least three different alarm calls to warn others about different kinds of danger. Bees perform elaborate dances to communicate information about food sources and distances, and male birds inform others of their impressive status by the length and variety of their songs. These and many other methods of communication are critical to these animals' lives, but these signals have fixed meanings and cannot be recombined to make new ones. In true language, arbitrary sounds or signs are combined in a potentially infinite number of ways to produce an equally vast number of possible meanings. These new combinations are then memes that can be copied from one person to another.

Attempts to teach language to other species have almost completely failed, despite some early hopes of success. There are several chimpanzees, gorillas, and orangutans who have learned American Sign Language, and some have vocabularies of several hundred signs. A gorilla called Koko even passed the mirror recognition test, suggesting that her training with sign language had other effects too, but mostly these apes use their signs to ask for food. They do not spontaneously set about naming things, playing with words, or telling everyone what they are up to, as young children do.

The relevance to consciousness is this. Some people argue that the addition of language completely transforms minds, bringing about the essentials of consciousness, including the sense of self, theory of mind, and the ability to think about past and future. In other words, without language no animal can be conscious, and since there is little or no evidence for language in other species we alone must be conscious. But how can we tell? If this problem seems difficult, it is nothing compared to the confusions surrounding the question of how, when, and why consciousness evolved in the first place.

The Function of Consciousness

Why are we conscious at all? You might argue that since we are conscious, consciousness itself must have had an evolutionary function.

At first sight this argument seems eminently plausible. The theory of evolution by natural selection is one of the great insights of science—simple, yet extraordinarily powerful. Some say it is the best idea anybody ever had. As Darwin realized, a simple reiterative process can create the most intricate and functional designs apparently out of nowhere. It works like this—start with something; make lots of copies of it with slight variations; select just one of these; and then repeat the process. That's all.

The power lies with the effect of selection. Darwin began by explaining artificial selection, in which people choose to breed from some animals and not others and in this way increase desirable characteristics, but he realized that the same process must operate with the blind processes of natural selection. That is, in a world with insufficient food, space, light, and air to go round, inevitably some creatures will do better than others, and whatever it was that helped them in the competition for survival will be passed on to their offspring, and so the process continues. As it does, characteristics such as eyes, wings, hair, and teeth all appear and evolve. These are the adaptations that helped the animals to survive, and will be passed on if they breed.

Is consciousness an adaptation? It might seem that it must be, because maladaptive characteristics are soon weeded out by selection, but there are two other main possibilities: consciousness might be a useless by-product, or it might be an inseparable component of something else that is adaptive (even if it does not appear to be). There are theories of consciousness of each of these three types but, as we shall see, they all land us in trouble.

Let's begin with what seems to be a perfectly natural idea—that we humans might have evolved without consciousness. In other words, consciousness is an optional extra, and we might all have been zombies. "Why not?" the argument goes. "I can perfectly well imagine a world in which people look just the same and behave just the same but inside there is no awareness, no 'what it is like' to be me." This intuition has fueled all sorts of thought experiments involving zombie twins, and even a complete zombie earth. But there is a serious problem.

Imagine a replay of evolution in which some of our ancestors were zombies while others were conscious—we can call them conscies. Natural selection now gets to work on this mixed population of zombies and conscies, and what happens? Absolutely nothing happens because, *by definition*, zombies are indistinguishable from conscies. They look the same, act the same, and say the same kinds of things. This means that natural selection would have nothing to work on. Any increase or decrease in zombies over conscies would be entirely random. This curious conclusion makes a nonsense of the idea that consciousness is an optional extra, a useless by-product, or an epiphenomenon. It is best to throw out the whole idea of zombies and move on.

This leaves two other possibilities: either consciousness is itself an adaptation, or it necessarily comes along with, or is an aspect of, other adaptations.

If consciousness is an adaptation, it makes sense to say that we might have evolved without it, but in this case we would not be philosophers' zombies; we would be more like Hollywood Haitian zombies—creatures deficient in something important, lacking in some crucial ability. Evolution would then have favored the conscies. If you take this view, you have to explain what it is that consciousness adds, and you will remember the trouble we had with the concept of consciousness actually doing anything. For a start, it is difficult to see how *subjective experiences* or *what it's like to be* could actually affect anything. Then there is all the evidence that the experiences come too late to be the cause of actions or to have the kinds of effects they are commonly thought to have.

Nevertheless, there are several theories of this kind. The most influential was proposed in the 1980s by psychologist Nicholas Humphrey. He argues that consciousness emerged in our ancestors because they were highly social animals with complex alliances and relationships. Individuals who could best predict the actions of others would be at an advantage, and the best way to do that is to evolve a kind of "inner eye" and observe yourself. In this way, the ability to introspect evolved and so we became conscious. This theory has been influential for the stress it puts on social intelligence and the origins of theory of mind. But as far as consciousness is concerned, it has been criticized on the grounds that introspection is a poor guide to behavior, the inner eye comes dangerously close to dualism, and the theory still does not account for *subjectivity*. Other theories have built on Humphrey's but face the same difficulty—understanding where subjectivity fits in and why the *experience itself* provides any selective advantages.

The third and final possibility is to throw out the idea that *experiences themselves* can do anything. In this view consciousness is not an adaptation, not because it is a useless by-product, but because it is not separable from intelligence, perception, thinking, self-concept, language, or any other evolved abilities. Perhaps a majority of materialist scientists think this way. They assume that somehow or other, when all these abilities are explained, we shall finally understand consciousness. The trouble is that this day seems far off. As yet there is no convincing theory to explain why having any of these abilities gives us a conscious

According to psychologist Nicholas Humphrey, consciousness emerged in our ancestors because they were highly social animals with complex alliances and relationships. Chimpanzees, our nearest living relatives, live in complex social groups as we do. They form and break alliances, make and lose friends, and keep track of who has treated them badly or well.

mental life—why *subjectivity* necessarily comes along with all the rest. This is not to say that this is impossible to explain, but until we can do so we shall keep lapsing back into believing in zombies and grappling with the hard problem.

We can now see that theories of the evolution of consciousness range from those that place its origin way back with the emergence of life itself, through intermediates linking it with the evolution of perception, intelligence, or other general abilities, to those that tie it to language, imitation, or memes. But no one yet agrees which is right nor—more importantly— has any idea how to find out.

• • • • •

MEMES

Memes are habits, skills, behaviors, or stories that are copied from person to person by imitation. Like genes, memes compete to be copied,
but instead of being chemicals locked inside cells, they are information that jumps from brain to brain, or from brains to computers,
books, and works of art. The winning memes spread across the world,
shaping our minds and cultures as they go.

Memes club together to make vast memeplexes. Many of these en-
hance our lives, such as financial systems, scientific theories, legal systems, and sports and the arts. But others are more like infections or
parasites that jump from host to host, such as quack remedies, cults,
chain letters, and computer viruses. Their basic structure is an instruction to "copy me" backed up with threats and promises.

Many religions use just this structure, which is why Richard Dawkins calls them "viruses of the mind." Roman Catholics are urged to
pass on the memes of their early indoctrination, especially to their
own children. Praying, saying grace at meals, singing hymns, going
to church, and contributing to impressive buildings all serve the in-
terests of these memes, and are encouraged with untestable threats of
everlasting hell and promises of heaven. Similarly, Islamic law protects
its memes by prescribing severe punishments for those who break the
faith. Belief without evidence is admired and doubt discouraged. A
religion's memes can therefore be successfully replicated whether or
not the central beliefs are true or valuable in any way. At the extreme
we find memes that kill their carriers, as in martyrs who die for their

faith, or that divert people's energy away from bringing up children in favor of spreading the memes, as in celibate priests. Traditional religions have largely survived by vertical transmission (parent to child). Memetic theory should allow us to predict how they will cope with increasingly fast horizontal transmission, and also which newly emerging religions and cults are likely to survive.

The self could also be a memeplex, a group of memes that thrive together and is strengthened every time the word *I* is used. Phrases such as *I want . . .* , *I believe . . .* , and *I know . . .* all fuel the false idea of a persistent inner self who has conscious experiences. Really there are just words being copied, and memes competing with each other to make us who we are—deluded meme machines.

· · · · ·

The Future of Consciousness

The confusion we have reached is deep and serious, and I suspect it reveals fundamental flaws in the way we normally think about consciousness. Perhaps we need to throw out the most basic assumptions and start all over again.

There are two really fundamental assumptions that almost everyone makes. The first is that experiences happen to someone, that there cannot be experiences without an experiencer. This need not imply a fixed or unchanging self, but it does imply that the "you" who is now conscious of reading this book is the same one who went to bed last night and woke up this morning. This has to be thrown out.

The second assumption is that experiences flow through the conscious mind as a stream of ideas, feelings, images, and perceptions. The stream may break, change direction, or be disrupted, but it remains a series of conscious events in the theater of the mind. The bottom line here is that if you ask "What is in Jim's consciousness now?," there must be a correct answer, because some of Jim's thoughts and perceptions are in the conscious stream while the rest are not. This has to be thrown out.

So we start again with a new beginning. The starting point this time is quite different. We start from the simplest possible observation. Whenever I ask myself "Am I conscious now?," the answer will always be "yes."

But what about the rest of the time? The funny thing is that we cannot know. Whenever we ask the question we get an answer—yes—but we cannot ask about those times when we are not asking the question. The situation is reminiscent of change blindness and the "grand illusion" theory of vision. With vision you can always look again, and every time you look you see a rich visual world. So you assume that it is always there. You can try to snatch a glimpse of something, but you can never see what it is like when you are not looking. It is like trying to open the fridge very quickly to see if the light is always on; you can never catch the light being off.

This is how the grand delusion of consciousness comes about. We humans are clever, speaking, thinking creatures who can ask ourselves the question "Am I conscious now?" Then, because we always get the answer "yes," we leap to the erroneous conclusion that we are always conscious. The rest follows from there. We imagine that at every waking moment in our lives, we must be conscious of something or other, because whenever we asked we found it was true. So we invent metaphors that fit this conclusion, such as theaters and spotlights and streams of consciousness. But we are wrong. Completely wrong.

The truth is that when we are not asking the question, there are no contents of consciousness and no one to experience them. Instead, the brain carries on, doing multiple things in parallel—as in Dennett's multiple drafts theory—and none of them is either in consciousness or out of it. Indeed, the whole idea of brain activity being conscious or unconscious can be dropped, and with it the problem of the "magic difference" between them.

Consciousness, then, is a grand delusion. It arises through asking such questions as "Am I conscious now?" or "What am I conscious of now?" In that moment of questioning, an answer is concocted: a now, a stream of experiences, and a self who observes it all appear together, and a moment later they are gone. Next time you ask, a new self and a new world are concocted, backward from memory. If you go on to believe that you always were conscious, and construct metaphors about streams and theaters, then you only dig yourself deeper and deeper into confusion.

In this new way of thinking about consciousness most of the old problems disappear. We do not need to explain how consciousness is produced by, or emerges from, the objective activity of the brain, because it does not. We do not have to explain the magic difference between brain activity which is conscious and that which is not, because there is no difference. We do not have to wonder how subjective experiences evolved or whether they have a function, because there is no stream of experiences—only a fleeting event that gives rise to a delusion.

In this view only creatures capable of being so deluded could be conscious in the way that we human beings are. This probably means that humans are unique, or very nearly so, because only they have language, theory of mind, self-concept and all the other factors that help to create the delusion. Other animals go about their lives creating passing perceptual worlds as they go—creating experiences, if you like, but not streams of experiences happening to anyone. They never ask themselves difficult questions that land them in confusion.

So what is it really like to be them? Perhaps there is something it is like to be each fleeting construction; the tangled branches rushing past as a bird lands on its perch; the pain of stretched muscles as a horse gallops or a rabbit leaps to safety; the feel of closing in on that insect as the bat's sonar guides its flight. But there is no true answer to the question "What is it like to be a bat?" any more than there is anything it is like to be us most of the time. There is only an answer when we ask the question.

Could computers ever be conscious? This has been another thorny question with a long and tangled history. Some argue that only biological entities can be conscious while others claim that it is the functions the computer carries out that are relevant, not what it is made of. On the delusional theory of consciousness the answer is simple. If any machine had language or memes or whatever it takes to be able to ask the question "Am I conscious now?" and concoct theories about its inner self and its own mind, then it would be as deluded as we are and think it was conscious in the same deluded way. Otherwise it would, like nonhuman animals, construct temporary perceptual worlds through its interactions with the environment, but never imagine it was experiencing them.

Taking this new approach, one big question concerns the nature of questioning. What does it mean for a creature, or a machine for that matter, to ask itself a question? One way to investigate this might be to study what goes on in the brain of a person who is deeply questioning in this way. Might the flowing and dancing patterns of brain activity come together in some way, or might there be special patterns or connections? Methods similar to those used to look for the neural correlate of consciousness (NCC) could be used to find out.

Another question is whether we humans can drop the illusions and experience the world without them. Those who practice certain kinds of meditation or mindfulness claim that we can. They say that the ordinary world falls apart and there are just experiences with no one experiencing them. What would the brain activity of someone in this state look like? If we found out we might be closer to understanding how the illusions come about. While there is no guarantee that this approach would necessarily be easier, or even possible, it is certainly different from the current approach.

Research subjects would need to be highly skilled. One possible technique is Zen meditation which, with its use of special stories or questions called koans, uses exactly the sort of questions that are relevant here: "Who am I?" "When is now?" "What is this?" Practitioners of this method can steadily maintain and explore a deeply questioning frame of mind. Others practice mindfulness, in which they try to stay alert, open and fully present in the moment, whether meditating or not. This apparently simple technique can, with long practice, give rise to a state in which phenomena arise and fall away but without any sense of time or place, and with no one experiencing them.

In this exploration of consciousness, scientists might study practitioners, but conceivably the same person could do both. Indeed, there are already some scientists who practice this way, and practitioners who study the science. This holds out the hope that science and personal practice might eventually come together to let us see clearly—dropping the delusions, penetrating the illusions of self and other, and leaving us with one world—no duality, and no one asking the question.

FURTHER READING

•

GENERAL BOOKS

All the topics in this book are covered in more detail in S. J. Blackmore, *Consciousness: An Introduction* (London: Hodder & Stoughton; New York: Oxford University Press, 2003), along with exercises, demonstrations, and an extensive list of references.

D. C. Dennett, *Consciousness Explained* (Boston, MA, and London: Little, Brown and Co., 1991) provides a deep and fascinating philosophical approach. For opposing views, see D. Chalmers, *The Conscious Mind* (Oxford: Oxford University Press, 1996), and J. Searle, *The Mystery of Consciousness* (London and New York: Granta Books, 1998).

For psychology and neuroscience, try F. Crick, *The Astonishing Hypothesis* (New York: Scribner's, 1994) (a strong reductionist view), and G. M. Edelman and G. Tononi, *Consciousness: How Matter Becomes Imagination* (London: Penguin, 2000). (In the United States, this is published as *A Universe of Consciousness: How Matter Becomes Imagination*, by Basic Books.) A. Zeman, *Consciousness: A User's Guide* (New Haven, CT: Yale University Press, 2002), is a good overview.

William James's two-volume classic is *The Principles of Psychology* (London: MacMillan, 1890), and for some fun reading try D. R. Hofstadter and D. C. Dennett (eds.), *The Mind's I: Fantasies and Reflections on Self and Soul* (London: Penguin, 1981).

JOURNALS

The two main print journals are the *Journal of Consciousness Studies* and *Consciousness and Cognition*.

WEB RESOURCES

Journal of Consciousness Studies online, http://www.imprint.co.uk/jcs.html

Online papers on consciousness: this is an excellent source of many classic and contemporary papers, all available in full online, provided by David Chalmers, http://www.u.arizona.edu/˜chalmers/online.html

Psyche, an electronic journal, http://psyche.cs.monash.edu.au/

Science and Consciousness Review, an electronic journal, http://www .sci-con.org/links.html

My Web site, with other links and online articles, http://www .susanblackmore.co.uk/

CHAPTER 1

For readings on the hard problem, see J. Shear (ed.), *Explaining Consciousness—The "Hard Problem"* (Cambridge, MA: MIT Press, 1997), pp. 9–30, and more generally on philosophy of mind, D. Chalmers, (ed.), *Philosophy of Mind: Classical and Contemporary Readings* (Oxford: Oxford University Press, 2002). Nagel's original paper on the bat is T. Nagel, "What is it like to be a bat?" *Philosophical Review* (1974), 83: 435–50. It is widely reprinted, including in Chalmers's anthology, where you can also find Block's paper on concepts of consciousness, and Dennett on qualia.

Zombies are discussed in D. Chalmers, *The Conscious Mind* (Oxford: Oxford University Press, 1996), and D. C. Dennett, *Consciousness Explained* (Boston, MA, and London: Little, Brown and Co., 1991). The *Journal of Consciousness Studies* devoted a special issue to zombies, vol. 2, part 4 (1995).

CHAPTER 2

For readings on NCCs, see T. Metzinger (ed.), *Neural Correlates of Consciousness* (Cambridge, MA: MIT Press, 2000). For books on neuropsychology, including brain damage and blindsight, see A. Damasio, *The Feeling of What Happens: Body, Emotion and the Making of Consciousness* (London: Heinemann, 1999); A. D. Milner and M. A. Goodale, *The Visual Brain in Action* (Oxford: Oxford University Press, 1995); V. S. Ramachandran and S. Blakeslee, *Phantoms in the Brain* (London: Fourth Estate, 1998); and L. Weiskrantz, *Consciousness Lost and Found* (Oxford: Oxford University Press, 1997). For synesthesia, see R. E. Cytowic, *The Man Who Tasted Shapes* (New York: Putnams, 1993).

CHAPTER 3

Libet's delay is discussed in most general books on consciousness, including those above and J. McCrone, *Going Inside* (London: Faber & Faber, 1999) and in his own book, B. Libet, *Mind Time: The Temporal Factor in Consciousness* (Cambridge, MA, and London: Harvard University Press, 2004). Critical discussions of timing, the cutaneous rabbit, and other experiments are in D. C. Dennett, *Consciousness Explained* (Boston, MA, and London: Little, Brown and Co., 1991).

For the various theories discussed here, see B. J. Baars, *A Cognitive Theory of Consciousness* (Cambridge: Cambridge University Press, 1988), which describes global workspace theory and supporting evidence; G. M. Edelman, *Wider than the Sky: The Phenomenal Gift of Consciousness* (London: Allen Lane, 2004); R. Penrose, *Shadows of the Mind* (Oxford: Oxford University Press, 1994); and K. R. Popper and C. Eccles, *The Self and Its Brain* (New York: Springer, 1977).

CHAPTER 4

A. Damasio, *Descartes' Error: Emotion, Reason and the Human Brain* (New York: Putnams, 1994). For the power of unconscious processing, see G. Claxton, *Hare Brain, Tortoise Mind: Why Intelligence Increases When You Think Less* (London: Fourth Estate, 1997). For filling-in, see D. C. Dennett, *Consciousness Explained* (Boston, MA, and London: Little, Brown and Co., 1991) and V. S. Ramachandran and S. Blakeslee, *Phantoms in the Brain* (London: Fourth Estate, 1998).

Change blindness and the grand illusion theory of vision are discussed in A. Noë (ed.), *Is the Visual World a Grand Illusion?*, a special issue of the *Journal of Consciousness Studies* (2002), 9(5–6), and reprinted as a book by Imprint Academic of Thorverton, Devon. Also see A. Mack and I. Rock, *Inattentional Blindness* (Cambridge, MA: MIT Press, 1998). Demonstrations can be viewed at http://viscog.beckman.uiuc.edu/djs_lab/demos.html and http://www.psych.ubc.ca/˜rensink/flicker/download/.

CHAPTER 5

For a simple introduction to ego and bundle theories, as well as the teletransporter thought experiment, see D. Parfit, "Divided minds and the nature of persons," in C. Blakemore and S. Greenfield (eds.), *Mindwaves* (Oxford: Blackwell, 1987), pp. 19–26. Opposing views on self are aired in a special issue of the *Journal of Consciousness Studies* reprinted as S. Gallagher and J. Shear (eds.), *Models of the Self* (Thorverton, Devon: Imprint Academic, 1999).

Good introductions to Buddhism are S. Batchelor, *Buddhism Without Beliefs: A Contemporary Guide to Awakening* (London: Bloomsbury, 1997) and W. Rahula, *What the Buddha Taught* (London: Gordon Fraser; New York: Grove Press, 1959).

Split-brain cases are described in M. S. Gazzaniga, *Nature's Mind* (London: Basic Books, 1992) and dissociation in E. R. Hilgard, *Divided Consciousness: Multiple Controls in Human Thought and Action* (New York: Wiley, 1986). Early cases, and James's own theory of self, are in W. James, *The Principles of Psychology* (London: MacMillan, 1890).

CHAPTER 6

For the debate on Libet's experiment, see B. Libet, "Unconscious cerebral initiative and the role of conscious will in voluntary action," *Behavioral and Brain Sciences* (1985), 8: 529–39, with commentaries in the same issue, 539–66, and 10: 318–21. The experiment is widely discussed, most critically in D. C. Dennett, *Consciousness Explained* (Boston, MA, and London: Little, Brown and Co., 1991).

The first table-tipping experiment is in M. Faraday, "Experimental investigations of table moving," *Athenaeum* (1853), no. 1340: 801–3; and for further examples and Wegner's theory, see D. M. Wegner, *The Illusion of Conscious Will* (Cambridge, MA: MIT Press, 2002).

CHAPTER 7

Overviews of the topics discussed here can be found in J. A. Hobson, *Dreaming: An Introduction to the Science of Sleep* (New York: Oxford

University Press, 2002); M. Jay (ed.), *Artificial Paradises: A Drugs Reader* (London: Penguin, 1999); R. M. Julien, *A Primer of Drug Action: A Concise, Nontechnical Guide to the Actions, Uses, and Side Effects of Psychoactive Drugs*, rev. ed. (New York: Henry Holt, 2001); and M. Earleywine, *Understanding Marijuana: A New Look at the Scientific Evidence* (New York: Oxford University Press, 2002).

For OBEs and NDEs, see S. J. Blackmore, *Dying to Live: Science and the Near Death Experience* (London: Grafton, 1993) and H. J. Irwin, *Flight of Mind: A Psychological Study of the Out-of-Body Experience* (Metuchen, NJ: Scarecrow Press, 1985).

For a practical guide to meditation, see M. Batchelor, *Meditation for Life* (London: Frances Lincoln, 2001); and for research, see M. A. West (ed.), *The Psychology of Meditation* (Oxford: Clarendon Press, 1987).

CHAPTER 8

The evolution of consciousness is discussed in most general books on consciousness, but see also N. Humphrey, *A History of the Mind* (London: Chatto & Windus, 1992); N. Humphrey, *The Mind Made Flesh: Frontiers of Psychology and Evolution* (Oxford: Oxford University Press, 2002); and E. M. Macphail, *The Evolution of Consciousness* (Oxford: Oxford University Press, 1998).

Research on animal minds is reviewed in M. D. Hauser, *Wild Minds: What Animals Really Think* (New York: Henry Holt and Co.; London: Penguin, 2000).

For memes, see R. A. Aunger (ed.), *Darwinizing Culture: The Status of Memetics as a Science* (Oxford: Oxford University Press, 2000) and S. J. Blackmore, *The Meme Machine* (Oxford: Oxford University Press, 1999).

INDEX

•

Page numbers in *italics* include illustrations and photographs/captions.

PICTURE CREDITS

•

Danil Vitalevich; 155: © Shutterstock/Eric Isselée; 161: © Shutterstock/ Kletr

EMMA SKURNICK: 110

JOLYON TROSCIANKO: 72; 73; 90

COURTESY OF WIKIMEDIA COMMONS: 13: Zombie/Upload by Jean-noël Lafargue; 19: Cartesian Theater/Upload by Jennifer Garcia (Reverie); 30: Necker cube/Upload by BenFrantzDale; 37: Ventral-dorsal streams/Upload by Lokal Profil; 63: Café wall/Upload by Fibonacci; 65: Portrait of Archimedes by Giuseppe Patania; 69: Blind spot test/Upload by Frisko; 80–81: Robocup/Upload by Pablo from Granada, España; 87: Buddha in Haw Phra Kaew/Upload by Tevaprapas Makklay; 115: Portrait of Michael Faraday by Thomas Phillips; 131: *Nightmare* by Nicolai Abraham Abildgaard; 135: *Cannabis sativa*; 136: Dorothy Short as Mary Lane in *Reefer Madness*; 148: Hammundes oak at Freidewald, Germany/ Upload by Rainer Lippert; 151: Green shield bug/Upload by Opoterser

BRIEF INSIGHTS

•

A series of concise, engrossing, and enlightening books that explore
every subject under the sun with unique insight.

Available now or coming soon:

THE AMERICAN
PRESIDENCY

ARCHITECTURE

ATHEISM

THE BIBLE

BUDDHISM

CHRISTIANITY

CLASSICAL
MYTHOLOGY

CLASSICS

CONSCIOUSNESS

THE CRUSADES

ECONOMICS

EXISTENTIALISM

GALILEO

GANDHI

GLOBALIZATION

HISTORY

INTERNATIONAL
RELATIONS

JUDAISM

KAFKA

LITERARY THEORY

LOGIC

MACHIAVELLI

MARX

MATHEMATICS

MODERN CHINA

MUSIC

NELSON MANDELA

PAUL

PHILOSOPHY

PLATO

POSTMODERNISM

RENAISSANCE ART

RUSSIAN LITERATURE

SEXUALITY

SHAKESPEARE

SOCIAL AND
CULTURAL
ANTHROPOLOGY

SOCIALISM

STATISTICS

THE TUDORS

THE VOID

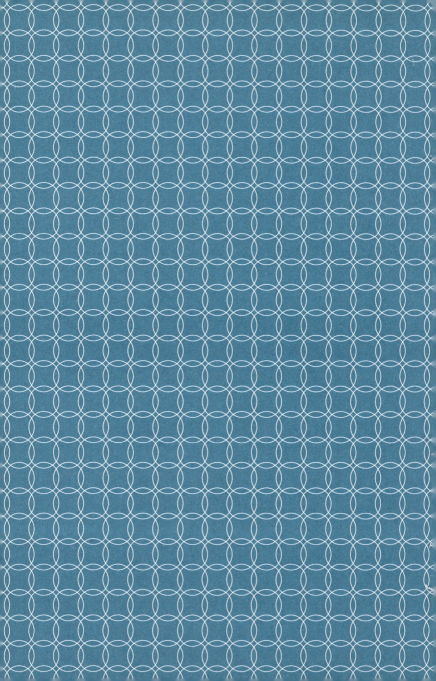